faithful

---
100 DEVOTIONS INSPIRED BY DOGS
---

paws

faithful paws

100 DEVOTIONS INSPIRED BY DOGS

Editors of *All God's Creatures*

Guideposts

A Gift from Guideposts

Thank you for your purchase! We want to express our gratitude for your support with a special gift just for you.

Dive into *Spirit Lifters*, a complimentary e-book that will fortify your faith, offering solace during challenging moments. Its 31 carefully selected scripture verses will soothe and uplift your soul.

Please use the QR code or go to **guideposts.org/spiritlifters** to download.

Faithful Paws: 100 Devotions Inspired by Dogs

Published by Guideposts
100 Reserve Road, Suite E200
Danbury, CT 06810
Guideposts.org

Copyright © 2025 by Guideposts. All rights reserved.

This book, or parts thereof, may not be reproduced, stored in a retrieval system, or transmitted in any form or by any means, electronic, mechanical, photocopying, recording, or otherwise, without the written permission of the publisher.

Cover and interior design by Beth Meyer
Cover photo by ti-ja. Interior images: p. 20–21, Thai Liang Lim; p. 42, urabazon; p. 43, ivanastar; p. 64, enduro; p. 65, xyom; p. 86, Youssef Edwar; p. 87, Alphotographic; p. 108, AnaSha; p. 109, Wiyada Arunwaikit; p. 130, alvarez; p. 131, Kanashi; p. 152, SensorSpot; p. 153, Danielle Mead; ; p. 174, MichaelSvoboda; p. 175, Jabez Corbett; p. 196, Nicolas Jooris-Ancoin; p. 197, yotrak.
Typeset by Aptara, Inc.

ISBN 978-1-961442-55-9 (hardcover)
ISBN 978-1-965859-00-1 (epub)

Printed and bound in the United States of America

Foreword

One of the joys of editing one of Guideposts' annual devotionals is working with the same writers year after year, hearing about their new discoveries, sharing their triumphs and their challenges as they move throughout the year. In this devotional made just for dog lovers, we've put together one hundred of our favorite devotions that feature our writers and their canine companions—the challenges, the lessons, and most of all, the love.

As you travel through the pages of this devotional, you'll meet some dogs in passing and follow others as they grow and learn along with their owners. We're especially excited to feature a series of devotions from Edward Grinnan, the editor in chief of *Guideposts* magazine, all centering on his special relationship with his golden retriever, Gracie.

But whether you read this book from beginning to end or just dip in when the mood strikes, we hope that you'll find as much joy and inspiration in reading this book as we did in putting it together.

Editors of *All God's Creatures*

Growing Pains

So we have not stopped praying for you since we first heard about you. . . . All the while, you will grow as you learn to know God better and better.

—COLOSSIANS 1:9-10 (NLT)

My phone rang at work the other morning. My wife, Julee. She was close to tears.

"She destroyed another pillow," Julee said. "There were feathers all over the living room. It looked like a hurricane hit a chicken coop."

I knew how she felt. Among the items Gracie, our adorable young golden retriever, has gleefully masticated are a number of TV remotes. Just that weekend I spent half of my Saturday waiting for the cable guy to show up so he could replace two more remotes that Gracie had attacked.

Gracie is as sweet and playful a dog as you will ever meet. But left to her own devices (I know, I know), Gracie will gnaw on almost anything—remotes, phone chargers, credit cards, cell phones, rugs, gloves, a shower curtain.

"When will she grow out of this?" Julee wailed before hanging up. I'd asked the Lord that same question, many times.

I got home that night and took Gracie to the park. I talk to my dogs, and I talked to her about my worries over her chewing. We found a bench and I invited her up. With a seventy-five-pound puppy sprawled across my lap, I sat there speaking and gesturing quite earnestly. Perhaps I looked crazy.

Suddenly, Gracie jumped up. I saw what she saw—one of those Styrofoam clamshell boxes that sandwiches come in. She tore off in its direction, me after her. All at once she veered away and fell upon a stick, taking it in her mouth and rolling happily on her back. A stick. This was progress! And a reminder: dogs do grow up eventually. We all do.

Edward Grinnan

Father, just as You have helped me grow up and out of temptation, I know You will guide my pets because You love all creatures.

Rescue or Puppy?

He gives food to every creature. His love endures forever.
—PSALM 136:25 (NIV)

It was an impossible choice: Adopt a rescue dog or pick out a puppy. At first, the answer had been clear. My husband, Brian, and I finally had a fenced-in backyard, and we could give a home to a dog in need. We monitored the rescue websites, waiting to find our perfect pup.

Finally, tired of waiting for direction or guidance, we headed to north Georgia, where one litter of puppies was ready to leave their mom. As we looked for the rural address, we got a call—a miracle, really, because we were in an area with little cell reception. It was the adoption agency telling us they had an eighteen-month-old golden retriever named Colby who was perfectly healthy, homeless, and ready to be loved. I told her we'd think about it as we pulled into the driveway of the puppies' house.

Brian and I spent the next hour surrounded by impossibly furry bundles of energy whose teeth were so small we couldn't even feel them gnawing on our shoes. We held them and snuggled them, and then we looked at each other and knew: these pups weren't for us.

We hopped in the car and headed for Atlanta, where we found Colby waiting for us. When we walked into the room, he came over and sat down between us, as if he'd known he was ours all along.

As I often do, I had tried to rush God's plan. I had tried to force a puppy to fit into the hole in our family that had been made just right for Colby. God allowed me to follow my own path but then gently nudged me back.

As we packed Colby into the car and headed home, he crawled into my lap, and I knew that this decision—God's decision—had been right all along.

Ashley Kappel

***Lord, help us know when it's time to adopt—
and when it's time to wait.***

Ten-Year Prayer

Rejoice always, pray continually, give thanks in all circumstances; for this is God's will for you in Christ Jesus.
—1 THESSALONIANS 5:16–18 (NIV)

*T**ime to give up praying*, I told myself sadly. My prayers were for someone I loved very much. But after ten years, they were still unanswered.

Later that afternoon, a letter to the editor in the local paper caught my eye. "Time to take down the 'Annie—Lost Dog' posters. Annie is back home!" I could hardly believe the amazing news. I'd prayed for Annie for nearly a year because her stubborn and desperate owner had refused to stop looking for her and to take his ad out of the paper. The ad had described Annie as very shy and feeling lost in unfamiliar surroundings, and said that she had run away during a visit to the owner's daughter in Athens, Georgia.

A few days later, the paper ran a full-length story with a picture of the black Labrador-retriever mix and her happy owner, who said he had simply refused to believe his dog wouldn't be found. He'd returned to Athens on weekends, walking the streets, calling for Annie late into the night, and sitting outside his daughter's home in thirteen-degree weather, hoping to get a glimpse of his pet. When the daughter begged her father to relinquish his hope of finding the dog and to begin the grieving process, he only intensified his prayers.

Ten full months after her disappearance, Annie was discovered, still wearing her identification tags, twenty-five miles from Athens. "I especially want to encourage others who have lost pets not to give up hope," Annie's ecstatic owner said.

Those last five words—not to give up hope—seemed to leap off the newspaper and land right in my heart. Laying the paper aside, I resumed my ten-year prayer.

Marion Bond West

Heavenly Father, help me draw my strength and hope from You as I face the trials of everyday life. Nothing is impossible in Your name. Amen.

Kindness of Strangers

Thou hast put gladness in my heart.
—PSALM 4:7 (KJV)

When my son took a job in Colorado, I inherited his cocker spaniel, Panda. She's loyal and affectionate, but she's a high-maintenance dog. Her floppy ears tend to get infections, and her sensitive digestive system calls for careful regulation of what she eats.

The pet store had a wide selection of books on the care of cocker spaniels. As I thumbed through a few of them, a young man came over and reached for a magazine. He grinned and said, "You have a cocker? I've had my Sandy since she was a puppy." That's all it took to get us talking. He had some great tips for Panda: use an antibacterial wash for her ears and do not give her table scraps. Then he handed me a dog-care manual. "This is the book I'd recommend. It covers just about everything. Good luck!" He looked at his watch and quickened his step as he walked to the cashier.

I sighed when I looked at the price on the cover. Expenses had been heavy recently, with a hefty vet bill for Panda. *But I really do need this*, I said to myself and added it to the dog food in my cart.

"So *you're* the lady," the cashier said as she separated the book from my supplies. "The tall blond guy paid for this. He said to tell you it was a gift to help you take good care of your cocker!"

I looked around, but he'd gone. "I didn't even know him!" I said. "How kind."

"He made my day too," said the cashier. Then she scooped up several small bags of dog treats and said, "Here are some freebies."

When I prayed that night, I thanked God for the joy of sweet surprises from the generous hearts of strangers.

Fay Angus

Lord, please watch over the people who show kindness to others. May they be blessed in turn.

Patience, Please

*The longer we wait, the larger we become,
and the more joyful our expectancy.*
—ROMANS 8:25 (MSG)

My dogs are not the cutest nor the smartest dogs around, but they are probably the world's best beggars. Oh, they are very polite about it. They just sit and stare as I consume a cookie or some other treat that they would love to have. They never bark or try to grab at a treat, they just sit patiently and wait. It doesn't matter how long it takes, as long as there is hope of getting a scrap, they will remain on duty in front of me waiting politely. Usually, their patience is rewarded because after all that waiting so nicely, I feel like sharing. I try to keep treat giving reasonable because dogs live longer with a healthy weight and lifestyle. If I gave in to their every whim, they would weigh a ton. Their health, along with their happiness, is important to me.

I once heard someone say that you can accomplish almost anything if you have patience. You can even carry water in a sieve if you wait until it freezes. Impatience, on the other hand, can have consequences. If my dogs give up and walk away, I no longer feel a need to save that last bite for them. As someone once said, "Many a man has turned and left the dock just before his ship came in."

Often God has us wait too. We pray and pray and it appears as if nothing is happening. God sees the big picture while our view is so limited. Sometimes it takes a while for God to work out the details and sometimes what we pray for is not in our best interests. It would be like me giving in to my dogs' desire to have treats 24/7. But God loves to share with those who remain faithful and continue to ask in prayer according to His will. It may take a while, but God will come through with the right answer at the right time.

Linda Bartlett

God above, let my patience outweigh my impatience as I wait on You. Amen.

Saved by Something You Can't See

Now faith is confidence in what we hope for and assurance about what we do not see.
—HEBREWS 11:1 (NIV)

He was lost. Anyone could see from the panic in this bedraggled dog's face that he had no idea how to get back to his home. Had he been dumped? Had he run in fear of a thunderstorm and become marooned far away from a place of security? Here he was in a loud and scary shelter after spending days and days on the run. His coat was dirty and matted. He was hungry, thirsty, and in need of much more care than a small rural shelter could afford.

But when the kind shelter attendant ran a scanner across the back of the terrified terrier, a miracle happened. A microchip tag revealed an owner in another state. A phone call and an email got an immediate response, and the loving family who had been looking for their baby promised to arrive the next day. A warm bath and a soft bed helped steady the little puffball a bit, but nothing could make him feel really safe until his family held their dog again in their arms. Something so tiny, something unseen and hidden inside the terrier, was its connection to home, to love, and to security.

We have the ability to embed a spiritual microchip as we hide God's Word in our hearts. This faith that no one else can see but that we can steadfastly rely on to bring God's open arms to us when we feel lost is beyond human understanding. Faith cements us to our God foundation when everything in the world tries to separate us and make us doubt his presence. Faith brings us a feeling of safety even in the darkest storms where strangers surround us. Faith keeps us from ever being truly alone, and it always brings us home.

Devon O'Day

Help me hide a spiritual microchip of Your love inside me, God, so that I never get lost.

Failing the Test

He is the one we proclaim, admonishing and teaching everyone with all wisdom, so that we may present everyone fully mature in Christ.
—COLOSSIANS 1:28 (NIV)

Training classes had gone pretty well with our one-year-old golden retriever, Petey. So I was surprised when, on the day of his therapy dog exam, he pulled on the leash, whipped his tail in a frenzy, and lunged to greet the other dogs waiting on the sidelines. This was definitely a therapy dog no-no. Petey failed his test.

I headed toward the door, disappointed. We'd always planned on Petey being a therapy dog, just like our older boy, Ernest. We'd socialized him, brought him to puppy play groups, and invested in training. I thought we were on the right track. Then, just like that, all our work went down the drain.

The dog trainer walked over and put her hand on my shoulder. "Don't feel too bad. Petey's a good dog. He has a great temperament. He just needs time to mature."

Isn't that just like my walk with Christ? I try to be obedient, but so easily become distracted and thrown off track. And then all my hopes and dreams for serving God seem so far out of reach. Yet a Christian life is one of maturing.

God doesn't care if I'm perfect. He cares more about the process. As long as I maintain a relationship with him, I'll continue learning and growing.

I knelt and hugged Petey tight. "It's OK. We'll keep working together. I love you." We'd practice every day, growing in knowledge and obedience.

Yep, both Petey and I had so much more to learn!

Peggy Frezon

Obedience and self-control isn't always easy. Sometimes I fail. But when I keep close to You, Lord, I gain maturity that strengthens me for the work You give me to do. Thank You! Amen.

Our Faintest Cry

***The righteous cry out, and the L<small>ORD</small> hears them;
he delivers them from all their troubles.***
—PSALM 34:17 (NIV)

My parents' dog, Sherry, was a wonderful mother. She constantly guarded and watched her pups when they were newborn. As they grew older, though she gave them more freedom, she continued to watch to ensure they didn't get hurt. And when they got into trouble, she was at their side in a flash to help or comfort.

After a while, with the puppies doing so well, Sherry returned to her normal practices she'd held before giving birth, such as sleeping on my parents' bed, which meant she left the pups in their bed in another room down the hall.

One night, one of her pups began to whimper and cry. Though the cry was faint, to her mama ears, it was as loud as a siren. Something was amiss and the puppy needed its mother. Sherry's head popped up and immediately she hopped off the bed and scurried to care for her baby.

Sherry exhibited a character trait of a good mother—but more so, she displayed a character trait of our Creator. Our God is always watching, guarding, and listening to us. There is no cry so faint that the Lord won't hear it; no worry or fear so trivial that he won't comfort; no pain so untimely that he will refuse to come quickly to our aid. For our God never sleeps. His eye is ever watchful and His ear ever hearing His children. We can be assured that, just as Sherry acted on her puppy's faint cry, when we are in distress, God will respond to our need; He never leaves us alone in our despair. What a comforting God we have!

Ginger Kolbaba

Thank You, Lord, for always watching over us, listening for our faintest cry.

Winston the Wanderer

"Suppose one of you has a hundred sheep and loses one of them. Doesn't he leave the ninety-nine in the open country and go after the lost sheep until he finds it?"
—LUKE 15:4 (NIV)

Winston, our terrier, loves to accompany my wife and me on hikes through the Colorado Mountains. Living life full on, his ears flopping in the wind, he leads the way.

On a crisp morning, we took an unfamiliar trail, passing rock walls on the right and sheer drops on the left. With no woods to explore, Winston ran ahead, out of sight.

Twenty minutes passed without his return. Panicked, we whistled. "Winston!" my wife called, tears streaking her face as she began to imagine what could have happened. "He's fallen, or worse, a bobcat . . . "

We heard a faint whimper overhead. "Stay here, in case he returns."

Walking around the base of the cliff looking for a way up, I wondered, *Is this how God feels when I wander? Do I cause him the same heartache?*

I struggled up the wall as the sandstone scraped my arms like glass. How often had God sacrificed all to chase after me? I'd always felt I had a short leash, but still I wandered. This lesson offered more than learning to watch my pet closer. God taught me his undying devotion to bring me back to his side.

Eventually, I reached the top, soaked with sweat. My wife called, "I have Winston!"

I looked over the edge, both relieved and annoyed.

"Not a scratch on him," she said. Winston's tail wagged as they cuddled.

Calmed, I sat a moment. Who knew I could care about a dog so much? It struck me again, the parallel between my love for Winston and God's love—and it warmed me.

Tez Brooks

Heavenly Father, thank You for never abandoning me. When I stray, You chase after me. Your love is relentless, and I'm grateful. Amen.

I picture each day as
if it were a happy dog
looking at me. I may not be
in the mood, but the
dog always wants to play.
Trust the dog.

JOHN PATRICK SHANLEY, PLAYWRIGHT

Learning the Limits

A soft answer turns away wrath, but a harsh word stirs up anger.
—PROVERBS 15:1 (ESV)

I'd had a long week, one that included several conflicts where I might have pushed people too hard when I should have backed off. It was a relief to take our young golden retriever, Gracie, to her favorite dog run.

Today she picked out a big yellow Lab to play with. It took her a minute or so to get Elijah interested, but that's Gracie for you. She's persistent when it comes to making friends. Soon she and her new pal chased a ball and ran after each other. Then they started to wrestle. Gracie was getting the better of Elijah when he snapped. Elijah lunged and snarled. Immediately both his owner and I were on our feet, separating the dogs before any damage could be done.

I assumed that the friendship with Elijah was over before it began. But eventually Gracie tried to get Elijah to play again, woofing at him and nibbling on his ear. As before, he couldn't resist. This time, just as Elijah was starting to get aggressive, Gracie backed off. She let Elijah calm down and then went back for more play. Again, just as he was reaching his boiling point, Gracie broke it off, galloping all the way around the perimeter of the run and barking happily. *How amazing*, I thought. *She figured out exactly Elijah's tipping point and then respected it so that he wouldn't get upset and they could remain friends.*

When Elijah's owner finally leashed him up to go, the big Lab strained to stay and play some more with Gracie. She gave him a playful swat as he was led away, and I gave my golden girl a big hug for teaching me a little something about how to play better with humans.

Edward Grinnan

Lord, teach me how to back off when things grow heated, to be guided by You instead of by my anger and frustration.

Commanded to Love

Dear friends, since God so loved us, we also ought to love one another.
—1 JOHN 4:11 (NIV)

When we moved from California to Wisconsin, my husband surprised me with a new puppy named Callie. The loving bundle of fur made me laugh and fended off loneliness with her adorable antics. Our fifteen-year-old dog, however, did not appreciate the change of climate in our new community or her new companion. She shunned the frisky, friendly addition to our family.

One day, our usually sweet and gentle senior dog grew tired of Callie's attempts to show her affection. Jazzy growled and retreated to her wire crate.

Callie plopped in front of the open crate, rested her chin on her front paws, and sighed.

"Oh, Jazzy," I said. "She just wants you to love her."

Jazzy glared at me, turned in circles, then curled up in the center of her crate.

After a while, I looked up from my work. Callie had waited for Jazzy to fall asleep and then snuck in to snuggle with her. With her back now pressed against one side of the crate, Callie had placed a paw on Jazzy's haunches.

As I prayed Jazzy would eventually warm up to the lovable pup, I considered how difficult our cross-country move had been on my husband and me. We didn't seem to fit in anywhere. Working from home and not being able to drive made it hard for me to make friends. With a list of churches to visit, I knew it would take time to develop relationships with our new church family.

So whenever I walked Callie after that, I started conversations with people. God grew a few of those casual interactions into genuine relationships. Eventually, He led us to a church family too. Though it's not always easy making new friends, God's great love for me fuels my willingness to love those who are different from me.

Xochitl Dixon

God, help me be open to new people who come into my life as others have welcomed me.

A Bond of Trust

How can a young person stay on the path of purity? By living according to your word. I seek you with all my heart; do not let me stray from your commands.
—PSALM 119:9-10 (NIV)

Blind since birth, my friend Michael Hingson escaped the 9/11 attacks on the World Trade Center by walking down seventy-eight flights of stairs with his guide dog, Roselle. When he heard what he described as a waterfall of falling glass from the first tower, Mike grabbed Roselle's harness, cried out to God for help, and just kept running with his dog. Their story hit the news quickly. Mike insisted that Roselle did not save his life that day; they did so as a team. Guide dog experts acknowledged that Roselle was special, but Mike's and Roselle's ability to read each other's cues and stay calm to the point of helping others testified to the unique bond between guide dogs and their handlers.

While coauthoring a children's book with Mike, I became fascinated with guide dogs and their extensive training. They begin learning commands as puppies and are regularly tested on their ability to focus and obey them. Less than 50 percent make it all the way through to graduation, but those that do make it possible for men and women who are blind to enjoy lives of independence and safety.

Our walk with God can resemble the guide dog–handler bond. From the moment we become believers, He begins teaching us and testing our ability to obey. The training is grueling and frustrating at times. Sometimes His Word tells us to do the exact opposite of what we want. But ultimately, His presence and guidance are lifesavers.

Jeanette Hanscome

Heavenly Father, I am grateful today that You don't force Your children to do life alone or without guidance. Thank You for filling Your Word with everything we need to know to live the life You gave us. Amen.

Ruby's Perfect Home

Be completely humble and gentle; be patient, bearing with one another in love.
—EPHESIANS 4:2 (NIV)

Some people find great deals the day after Christmas. We did, too, one year—but we didn't have to leave home to do the shopping or even go online.

As we've done many times, my husband, Craig, and I invited friends over to our home the day after Christmas for leftovers, dessert, and bluegrass. After jamming to Gospel tunes for hours, Steve and Betsy shared how they had picked up Ruby, an Australian red heeler, at a country crossroads with no homes or businesses for miles. Parents of five kids and numerous dogs, they thought nothing of bringing her home to their house next to a creek in our valley.

But Ruby's breed made her unhappy about sharing her new owners with other canine members of the family. Making matters more challenging, the family was going on a vacation and did not want to leave her with people strange to her, as well as the other dogs.

"We're looking for someone," Steve said, "who might take her for a week or so on a trial basis with the possibility of adopting her."

I looked at my husband. He was not shaking his head. And then after a long pause, he said, "Sure."

I knew what this meant: we were the owners of a red heeler. Forget the trial period. My husband had a new ranching partner.

She wasn't the friendliest of pets, with a grandchild or two nipped over the years, but she had a strong work ethic and proved to be a great ranch dog.

The same is true for people. Some simply do not have social tendencies. They may be reserved in nature or insecure in public settings or even rather contrary. However, each person has worth, and we can appreciate them and their gifts nonetheless.

Janet Holm McHenry

Lord, help me see beyond someone's crusty exterior so as to value his or her unique qualities. Amen.

The Bread of Life

And Jesus said to them, "I am the bread of life. He who comes to Me shall never hunger, and he who believes in Me shall never thirst."

—JOHN 6:35 (NKJV)

Our first family dog arrived when I was eleven. A Chihuahua-and-who-knows-what mixture, Taco was tiny enough to curl up in my cupped hands. A sweet boy from the start, Taco let me dress him up in my doll's clothes, only looking mildly embarrassed. My brothers played fetch with him. He never tired.

Though not the usual hound, my dad took him hunting. When Daddy wanted to scout an area, he mounted his motorcycle and tucked Taco inside his leather jacket, doggie-face peeking out, and off they went. Should the dog need to stretch his legs, he ran alongside the bike. When he jumped against Daddy's leg, it was jacket time.

We each knew Taco loved us. But he loved Mother most, though she had little time for dogs during her busy days. He followed her around as if she was his favorite human. When she drove into town to shop for groceries,

Taco trotted to the end of the driveway and parked himself. He waited there until Mother returned. Happy again, he tailed her like a detective, as usual.

No matter how much I pampered Taco, he still preferred Mother. One day I asked her why. Her response was a spiritual lesson for me.

"He doesn't love me best because I pay him attention. Taco just knows where his next meal comes from, so he keeps an eye on me. I'm the one who feeds him."

How wise to follow after Jesus as faithfully as Taco pursued Mother. She fed him life-giving food. Jesus is the true bread from heaven. If we believe in Him, the food He gives leads to not only life abundant, but life eternal.

Cathy Elliott

***Lord, may I never hunger for the bread
only You can provide.***

Love Letters

But I am like an olive tree flourishing in the house of God; I trust in God's unfailing love for ever and ever.
—PSALM 52:8 (NIV)

Josie is a tough girl. She had a tough life before I met her. This is often the case for dogs that come through rescues and shelters. If only they could tell us their stories.

When Josie looks at me now, after years of being loved and safe and cared for, I can see that there is a love that she tries so hard to express. She will sit obediently by my leg as I sit on the couch, but if my hand leaves her head, she softly lays a paw on my knee to remind me that a simple touch is a powerful gesture of love. She needs that gesture constantly.

What would Josie write in a letter to me if she had the ability to express her feelings in words? What would her love letter say? I know that my love letter to her would read something like this:

Dear Josie,

You are the best dog anyone could ever have. You do not have to prove yourself to me. You are loved. I do not know how to convince you of that love any more than I already have. It seems that sometimes, Josie, you are afraid that you will do something or have done something that will make me not love you. My dear, tough girl, there is nothing you could do to make me not love you. How do I get you to understand that? You do not have to compete for my love. I have enough for you always. There is no one that holds your place in my heart.

Then it occurred to me that these same words might be in her letter to me. And I melted as I realized that this is in God's love letter to me, too. It is in God's love letter to you as well.

Devon O'Day

May every one of my days be a love letter to You, Lord.

Someone Who Understands

I know what I'm doing. I have it all planned out—
plans to take care of you, not abandon you,
plans to give you the future you hope for.
—JEREMIAH 29:11 (MSG)

I loved volunteering at the no-kill dog shelter. If you want unconditional love just for showing up, try it sometime. But after a few months, I noticed the downside of a shelter that kept all its members until they found a home. Some dogs were hard to place and remained at the shelter much longer than they should.

Such was the case with JoJo, one of the Dalmatian pups I had worked with since birth. Her littermates went home one by one, but JoJo remained. She had been at the shelter for more than two years and had become fearful of the outside world. We would take her to meet and greets at pet stores only to have her cower in the back of her kennel and howl. It made finding a home difficult.

Until the right client came along, that is. One afternoon, Carolyn came in searching for the right pet. She was newly divorced and fearful of the future. She wanted a pet that would understand. She visited JoJo and sat near her cage for two weeks before she finally dared take JoJo for a walk. JoJo didn't whine or howl. Carolyn took JoJo for another walk the next day and the following five days until JoJo gained confidence. Carolyn kept up her vigil until JoJo trusted her completely. A month later, she took JoJo home.

Carolyn felt broken and fearful but determined to help a dog that felt the same. It is extra wonderful to see a dog that had lost hope regain it and find a forever home. We are often broken and fearful too, but God has the patience and determination to move us forward if we let Him. God must be extra joyful, too, when we lean upon Him to face the future.

Linda Bartlett

Heavenly Father, take my brokenness and make me whole again. Let me trust You completely. Amen.

Hospice Dog

"Blessed are those who mourn, for they shall be comforted."
—MATTHEW 5:4 (NIV)

One email stood out—a caregiver requesting a therapy dog visit for her father in hospice. I hesitated—our golden retriever was a therapy dog, but this wasn't the kind of visit that was easy. I found it difficult to remain positive and encouraging when I knew a patient's days were numbered.

Yet I remembered the day we made exactly such a request. My father-in-law, Ed, was in hospice. Ed had a special relationship with one of our dogs, Moses, and I longed to bring his pal to visit. But Moses no longer lived with us. Another dog in our house didn't get along with him, and we'd made the difficult decision to return Moses to Kathy, his foster mother. I felt sorry I couldn't give Ed the pleasure of running his hands across Moses's soft fur one last time.

Then I decided to call Kathy. "Would you mind bringing Moses over?" I explained the situation. They arrived the next day.

Ed lay in bed. "Moses is here to see you," I said. Although he hadn't done so in weeks, Ed lifted his head and tried to sit up. My husband helped guide his father's hand to the dog's neck. Ed's eyes twinkled, and a smile spread across his face. He patted Moses's soft fur.

It couldn't have been easy for Kathy to be there that day. But she knew her selfless act brought comfort to Ed. To all of us. The kind of comfort God brings us in our most difficult times.

I rubbed my dog's ears and thought of the caregiver's email. "Yes," I wrote back. "We'll be there."

Peggy Frezon

Dear Lord, I pray that those in need today will be open to receiving Your comfort, joy, and peace. I may not know their troubles, but You do. Amen.

Following Stubby's Example

__Praise be to the God and Father of our Lord Jesus Christ . . . who comforts us in all our troubles, so that we can comfort those in any trouble.__

—2 CORINTHIANS 1:3-4 (NIV)

The retired Army chaplain opened his Memorial Day speech by sharing an anecdote about Stubby, the most famous dog of World War I. In 1917, when an American soldier named Robert Conroy was shipped overseas with the 102nd Infantry, he smuggled Stubby onboard. Even though the dog had no training, Stubby proved to be a good soldier. When a German spy tried to sneak into camp, Stubby attacked the man's leg and wouldn't let go until the Americans captured him.

Another night, Stubby barked incessantly, waking up Conroy and the other sleeping soldiers. The Germans were launching a gas attack! The men quickly put on their gas masks, realizing the dog's warning had saved their lives.

Between battles, Stubby cuddled up next to wounded men. He licked their faces, trying to cheer them up. Grateful soldiers pinned their own medals to his collar.

Nurses made Stubby a little blanket to wear. Soon that was covered with medals and ribbons too.

After serving in seventeen battles together, Conroy and Stubby returned to the United States. By then, Stubby was famous and an honorary member of the American Red Cross, the YMCA, and the American Legion. In the years following the war, he met three US presidents and took part in more parades than any other dog in the world.

As I listened to the chaplain, I realized that like Stubby, I don't need special training to be of assistance to others. I can lend a hand or lend an ear. I can offer comfort and a casserole. Simply by caring and paying attention, I can be a blessing to others.

Shirley Raye Redmond

Lord, thank You for providing people and animals in my life who give me comfort and help. Help me to offer the same to others. Amen.

A Time for Everything

***There is a time for everything, and a season
for every activity under the heavens.***
—ECCLESIASTES 3:1 (NIV)

One night, my family and I had dinner in a restaurant with a friend who had been diagnosed with PTSD after serving in Vietnam.

I couldn't help but admire our friend's service dog, who lay quietly next to him. "He's so well behaved."

"That's because he's wearing his vest," our friend explained, referring to the bright yellow "service dog" vest. "When the vest is on, he's working."

"Is he this well behaved even without the vest?" I asked, unconvinced that a vest made that much of a difference. The dog was so calm it was hard to imagine him being anything but that docile.

My friend chuckled. "Oh no, without the vest, he's very playful, a regular dog. He just knows the difference."

I shook my head in amazement. Even his dog understood the difference between work and play. "I could take a lesson from that dog!" I said, laughing.

Perhaps we all could. How often do we unintentionally confuse our timing? When we're in mourning, for instance, would we rather be dancing? And yet the Bible tells us that each "time" is assigned for a purpose and therefore is good.

The dog knows that play will come—when it's time. We can know too that good "times" will come for us as well—when it's time. And in the meantime, we can lean into the season we are in—even those that are difficult—knowing we are in it for a purpose.

Ginger Kolbaba

Father, help me to lean into those difficult times with the reassurance that they serve a purpose. Amen.

Perhaps dogs help us remember the depth of our roots, reminding us—the animals at the other end of the leash—that we may be special, but we are not alone. No wonder we call them our best friends.

PATRICIA B. McCONNELL, AUTHOR

I Need Your Assurance

*I say, "Loyal love is permanently established;
in the skies you set up your faithfulness."*
—PSALM 89:2 (NET)

"**G**racie, no!"

My young golden retriever was trotting into the living room, a dish towel in her mouth. She'd captured it from the handle on our fridge. She stared at me, uncertain she was ready to surrender it.

"Gracie, drop!" I said, my voice firmer. Another second or two of deliberation, then she dropped the purloined towel gently on the floor and proceeded to her bed, where she curled up and sighed.

Gracie loved putting things in her mouth. It was a habit my wife, Julee, and I were determined to curb. A few minutes later, my dog's cold, wet nose nudged my hand. Julee, coming into the room, said, "I heard you scold her. I think she wants to make up."

"Maybe she wants to play or something," I said.

"Maybe that's what she wanted in the first place. She was just trying to get your attention."

I fought off a pang of guilt. She nudged my hand again, and I put my arm around her. Julee was right, though. Gracie needed reassurance. We were her family, and she needed to know everything was all right. Do dogs feel and think, much like we humans do? You bet they do.

"Get your ball," I said to Gracie. She leaped up, tail wagging excitedly, went to her toy box, and, after clearly thinking it over, picked out her favorite ball. We were off to the park. Mission accomplished, from my dog's point of view.

Edward Grinnan

Father, how often we seek Your reassurance when we feel we have failed You! It is the enduring grace of Your love that reassures use we are never forsaken.

More Grateful

***God decided in advance to adopt us into
his own family by bringing us to himself
through Jesus Christ. This is what he wanted
to do, and it gave him great pleasure.***
—EPHESIANS 1:5 (NLT)

Before we adopted our first rescue, I'd always dismissed statements like "rescue dogs make the best pets" or "somehow they just seem more grateful" as romanticizing. *That's silly,* I'd think. *A dog is a dog.*

Then Winston joined our family. He was a freckle-faced spaniel with curly ears and a feathery tail that he waved like a flag in a parade. Unlike our previous dog, a purebred cocker with a snobby sense of entitlement, Winston enthusiastically received anything and anyone. I'd toss him a paper towel roll to shred, and he'd act like it was Christmas. A plastic soda bottle to roll around the yard? Coolest thing he'd ever seen. He gobbled treats like manna from heaven and ate his meals with enthusiasm and abandon. Sitting beside me, he'd lay his silky head on my lap, close his eyes, and exhale a deep sigh of doggy joy.

"David," I said to my husband, "I think it's true. Winston does seem more grateful. I think he remembers what it was like before he was adopted, when he was hungry, sick, and abandoned. He doesn't take anything for granted."

Winston and I have a lot in common. Like my furry friend, I was hungry, sick, and abandoned in my sin. But God adopted me. He fed me with spiritual food, healed my sin-sick soul, and welcomed me into His family. And every day, He fills my life with good things. It's only fitting, then, that I live a life of gratitude.

I can almost imagine the angels in heaven looking down on the inhabitants of Earth and saying, "Rescued humans make the best people. Somehow they just seem more grateful."

Lori Hatcher

Lord, help me never forget how You rescued me, healed me, and adopted me into Your family. May I be ever grateful for the good and perfect gifts You bless me with every day. Amen.

The Pet Connection

"The King will reply, 'Truly I tell you, whatever you did for one of the least of these brothers and sisters of mine, you did for me.'"
—MATTHEW 25:40 (NIV)

I met Sheila when her dog, Buddy, was off-leash and ran over to greet me. I quickly started noticing a pattern: whenever I knelt to pet Buddy, Sheila would start talking . . . and talking. I loved Buddy, but some days I didn't have time to talk, and her topics so often turned negative. So sometimes I planned my walking routes to avoid them.

"I think she uses her dog as bait," I told my family.

But I began to feel the Holy Spirit's nudging about my attitude. I eagerly stopped to talk to other dog owners. There was Erika, whose cute schnauzer greeted me with happy barks when we passed each other on walks. Gracie, whose shaggy breed I could never remember, sat pristinely in front of our neighbor Esther's house, waiting for affection; I enjoyed catching up with Esther through Gracie. But I avoided Sheila and Buddy. Yes, Sheila was hard to get away from and had a reputation for being "off." But was that a valid excuse to snub her? One day, I saw her and Buddy and realized: *All she has is that dog and her neighbors. If she didn't use Buddy as bait, nobody would notice her.* Was it possible that Jesus would consider her "one of the least of these"?

Buddy rushed over. I knelt to pet him and said hi to Sheila.

Pets allow us to connect with wonderful people and some we'd rather not deal with. Jesus's words can inspire us to see otherwise invisible people and regard our encounters with them as opportunities to minister to them as if they were Jesus Himself.

Jeanette Hanscome

Jesus, it's one thing to have boundaries and another to be rude. Remind me not to neglect those You care about either. Help me to see each person I meet as a chance to represent You. Amen.

Love Serves

In fact, this is love for God: to keep his commands.
—1 JOHN 5:3 (NIV)

After I moved from California to Wisconsin, my new doctor informed me that pain management may be the best he could offer me. Though I grieved the possibility of living with severe chronic pain caused by an impact injury to my upper back, I found hope in the puppy we adopted when we moved to the Midwest.

Callie makes me feel less alone. She kisses my tears away and makes me laugh. She comforts me, snuggling closer to me when I'm hurting. She even encourages me to walk, which has improved my health, both physical and spiritual. But when I announced I wanted to train Callie to be a service dog, a friend said she couldn't be a good service animal because I love her too much.

The trainer I'd contacted immediately quashed that misconception. He said, "The love-bond you share with her will make her a better service dog. She'll obey you because she loves you and wants to please you."

As my tears flowed, I praised the Lord and recognized a deep spiritual truth in our trainer's statement.

The apostle John describes our obedience to God as an expression of our love for Him. When we personally experience God's unconditional and sacrificial love for us, He'll help us realize the trustworthiness of His character. He'll help us recognize His commands and His motives as loving and good. Like my sweet Callie, our obedience will be a loving response as we serve our loving master.

Xochitl E. Dixon

Loving Father, thanks for loving us and empowering us to love You by following Your lead. Amen.

Coming from Nothing

In the midst of a very severe trial, their overflowing joy and their extreme poverty welled up in rich generosity.
—2 CORINTHIANS 8:2 (NIV)

In rescue shelters, you see how animals can come from horrific situations and still have a beautiful heart.

Diesel was a brindle pit bull with scars across his face and body that were symbols of his life as a bait dog. His big jaws smiled when anyone walked past. And when he wagged his tail, it hit the wall of his run so hard that it split, requiring a white bandage at the tip. This didn't stop his smiling and wagging. When he was found wandering the streets, his ribs were sticking out from his side like a xylophone and it was obvious he was starving and cold.

As a bait dog, Diesel was used in fights to train the fighters, leading to regular, severe injuries. His survival alone is a miracle. When he was rescued, Diesel was homeless, hungry, yet the happiest dog you would ever meet. At playtime, he always took a toy to the new animals. He would not eat until all the other dogs were also eating. And if there was a spot on his bed, he welcomed others to join him and curled around them in a secure hug.

Diesel was a sharer. He taught me that generosity comes not from all we have, but from the heart that welcomes others in. I learned that sometimes those who have been blessed with much can hold tightly in fear of losing those things, while those who come from nothing realize that sharing in love brings the true blessing.

Devon O'Day

God, help me share freely what You have provided and let the love interest from that investment grow my heart.

The Persistent Prayer Poodle

One day Jesus told his disciples a story to show that they should always pray and never give up.
—LUKE 18:1 (NLT)

I wasn't a fan of the toy poodle a caring friend gave my children when they were small. Owachee was a high-maintenance pup, given to howling when my youngest cried and requiring costly grooming. But, as they say, free is free, and my children adored all five pounds of him.

One February night, I let him outside to handle his business before we all turned in. Moments later, he was gone.

We searched to no avail. My children were inconsolable, especially when daylight arrived and their beloved dog still hadn't turned up. We did all we could to find him, but weeks passed, and no one called.

My husband and I assumed a coyote had mistaken him for chow, but my children refused to give up hope. Nightly, they prayed for the poodle's safe return. After a month, I tried to manage their prayer expectations, but they wouldn't have it. They persisted.

Come June, we discussed finding a new dog. My youngest pouted that we'd "given up faith." Two nights later, my husband answered the phone and turned to me, amazed. "That was a woman thirty miles from here. Owachee wandered into her yard, and he's fine." (In fact, he'd gained two pounds and was still wearing our tags.) We'll never know how he spent the better part of five months, but my daughter didn't care.

"Ha!" exclaimed my daughter, "I told you God was listening! I never did give up, did I?"

Part of me wanted to tell her that every dog isn't found, and every prayer isn't answered, but I was too much in awe of what God had done in response to the persistent prayers of a child.

Lori Stanley Roeleveld

Lord, sometimes I get caught up in my own expectations instead of persevering in prayer as You taught us to do. Help me come to You with a persistent, childlike faith, and prepare for a surprise.

It Takes a Village

Two are better than one, because they have a good return for their labor: If either of them falls down, one can help the other up. But pity anyone who falls and has no one to help them up.
—ECCLESIASTES 4:9-10 (NIV)

Our boxer dog, McKenzie, was pregnant, and so was I. McKenzie was feeling particularly maternal, often trotting over to me to lay her head on my belly. She seemed to know that we were in this together.

McKenzie's puppies came first. We knew how many she should be delivering, but she seemed distressed toward the end. At the emergency animal clinic, she received help to deliver the rest.

We loved having those sweet puppies, but then we began to notice that Mama McKenzie wasn't able to feed them all. Our vet taught us how to push tiny tubes down tiny throats to provide nutrition. My brother-in-law was recruited for daytime feedings. My husband and I groggily handled the night shift. Our vet took care of the smallest puppy. Our small village of helping hands made the difference. After a few months, we couldn't believe how great they looked. Chubby rolls replaced skinny tummies and exploring legs replaced listlessness.

When I had pregnancy complications and delivered my son prematurely, the helping hands of friends and family gathered around my own tiny baby. Making meals, holding the baby, bringing coffee, and coming over to chat were gifts to me from those I loved. My life is infinitely better when surrounded by trusted people that jump up to help whenever needed. Two—or more—are definitely better than one.

Twila Bennett

Thank You, Lord, for dear friends who have been beside me for decades. You knew exactly who to bring into my life at exactly the right times. I couldn't do life without them. Amen.

Safe in My Father's Arms

For I am convinced that neither death nor life, neither angels nor demons, neither the present nor the future, nor any powers, neither height nor depth, nor anything else in all creation, will be able to separate us from the love of God that is in Christ Jesus our Lord.

—ROMANS 8:38-39 (NIV)

We have an adorable one-year-old miniature schnauzer named Gabriella. She is as sweet as an angel, and she earns her nickname, Gabby, when she talks to us with her distinctive voice.

She is the most lovable and cuddly dog ever, but she is afraid of scary sounds. When you're only twelve pounds, there are all kinds of things that constitute *scary*—from the doorbell ringing, to the wind blowing, to her toy squeaking, to a truck driving by . . .

As frightened as she may be, she stands her ground, barking at whatever has startled her and warning them away. It's only when my husband calls her name, and she leaps into the safety of his arms that she's able to settle down.

"You're safe, sweetheart," my husband will say as she cuddles into his strong arms. She trusts him completely, and before you know it, she's sound asleep.

If I'm honest, there's a lot in this world that frightens me, as well—illness and health concerns affecting me and those I love, getting enough work, financial concerns and being left all alone in this world, among others. Yet God promises we won't ever be left truly alone in this world. He cares for every aspect of our lives. This knowledge leaves me to trust the Lord to see me through no matter what the future holds. Like Gabby, I can face the scary sounds in my life because I have strong arms into which to run.

Deb Kastner

Lord, help me remember You are always with me, Your wisdom guiding me no matter what is happening in my life. Help me to respond to those scary sounds by running into the safety of Your arms. Amen.

Love Isn't Always Pretty

*The LORD is a refuge for the oppressed,
a stronghold in times of trouble.*
—PSALM 9:9 (NIV)

My first "client" at the no-kill dog shelter was so ugly that he made a warthog look beautiful. Spanky had short, stubby legs; a long, solemn face; a crooked tail; and a rotund body. He looked like someone had taken leftover dog parts and stuck them together. Spanky was surrendered to the shelter because his owner could no longer care for him. He was nothing in the looks department, but he had been loved. The sad thing is that the price for that love was grief, and Spanky was definitely in mourning. The staff wanted me to comfort him whenever he howled, and so I loved on him and took him for short walks.

He hadn't been exercised for a while due to his owner's handicaps, but once Spanky strengthened his legs a bit he began to relish his weekly walks. He also enjoyed chasing balls in the play yard. With all of these activities, he began to experience joy again. He began to show his true heart and beautiful soul. I forgot he was ugly.

Spanky was very social and the staff knew he was ready for a kennel mate. They found a cute little poodle to share Spanky's space, and the two hit it off well. Spanky was actually happy again. I worried for him though, thinking his new friend was darling and likely to be adopted quickly. I dreaded the thought of Spanky alone again.

Imagine my surprise when I returned to the shelter one day and found Spanky's cage empty. I could see Spanky's partner being adopted but never dreamed that someone was kind enough to hear Spanky's story and take both dogs. I had worried about Spanky needlessly. No doubt Spanky repaid his new owner tenfold with love and loyalty. My faith in humankind was renewed that day.

Linda Bartlett

Father of all, may I trust You through grief in this life to find my way back to joy in Your time. Amen.

Coming Out of My Shell

For the Spirit God gave us does not make us timid, but gives us power, love and self-discipline.
—2 TIMOTHY 1:7 (NIV)

Walking down our country road with my Pomeranian poodle mix, Piper, I spotted something moving in the road. When I got closer, I realized that it was a baby turtle. It was so tiny—its shell was only an inch across—and it had gotten turned upside down, so its little legs were flailing through the air.

Poor guy, I thought as I bent to turn the turtle over. Before I reached it, Piper scooped it up in her mouth. "Put him down," I shouted. "He's not food."

I tried to grab her, but she darted away. She ran to the side of the road and gently set the turtle down in the grass. She nudged it with her nose a few times, flipping it right side up. The turtle remained still, its head and legs pulled into its shell. Piper nudged the little creature again, but it still didn't move. I realized that the tiny turtle was frozen in fear, and it probably wouldn't move as long as we were nearby, watching.

"Let's go, Piper," I said, tugging gently on her leash. "You did what you could to help him, and now he has to decide for himself to move forward."

That afternoon, I received an invite to an event where I wouldn't know many people. I didn't want to go. Then I realized I was acting like that little turtle. Frozen by the fear of rejection or failure, I hide in my own shell, instead of moving forward toward the things I want. My fear stops me from applying for that new job or inviting a new acquaintance out for coffee. It's easy for me to stay in my comfort zone. But when I poke my head out of my shell, I see that God has surrounded me with people to encourage me and help me, just like Piper did with the turtle.

Diane Stark

Lord, show me one small, brave step I can take today to bring myself out of my shell.

The world would be a nicer place if everyone had the ability to love as unconditionally as a dog.

M. K. CLINTON, AUTHOR

Love Is Never Easy

Beloved, let us love one another, for love is of God.
—1 JOHN 4:7 (NKJV)

The two-mile trek up Monument Mountain in Great Barrington, Massachusetts, is a ritual adventure for me and all the dogs I've loved. Especially Gracie, our three-year-old golden retriever. It is her favorite place in the world. She's not a huge fan of the car, but when we head toward Monument Mountain, she nudges me from the back seat, tail a-wag, as if to speed us along.

The other day, a hot sunny morning, we stopped halfway up the mountain at a cherished trail juncture so we could both have a drink. I rested my sunglasses on a rock and busied myself getting her portable water bowl out and filled after stealing a peek at my work email on my phone (I know better, but I did it anyway). Meanwhile Gracie scurried off into some undergrowth, her hindquarters to me. *Wonder what she found?*

"Gracie, come get a drink."

She didn't come right away. She bolted up the trail instead and then darted back to lap sloppily at her bowl, glancing up at me. A group of hikers passed by, greeted cheerily by my golden. Then we were on our way. Except I couldn't find my sunglasses. My new, pricey prescription sunglasses. I knew at once: Gracie.

I searched for five minutes before I found the mangled remains a few yards up the trail, gnawed nearly beyond recognition and then crushed underfoot by the recent hiking party. There had been intent. There had been deceit and concealment.

"How could you?" I wailed, shielding my eyes to better glare at her. She had moved on up the trail by now, tail aloft, while I clutched the remnants of my glasses. I wanted to scream—or to weep. Instead I laughed. *No*, I thought, *love is never easy*. If it were easy, it wouldn't be love. Maybe that was the lesson on this hot sunny day.

Edward Grinnan

Dear God, keep teaching me to love when love is the hardest.

Letters to Ernest

For the entire law is fulfilled in keeping this one command: "Love your neighbor as yourself."
—GALATIANS 5:14 (NIV)

It was the last day of the school year, and the first-grade class gathered around. Although filled with joy as they anticipated the impending summer vacation, the students were also sad to say goodbye to their book buddy, our golden retriever, Ernest. We had brought him in regularly for story time, when the kids practiced their reading skills as he lay at their sides and listened.

On this last day, the students had written letters to Ernest, expressing what he had meant to them. Ernest sat attentively, his golden head on the child's lap, as each child read a heartfelt note. I found myself tearing up at their words: *You are nice to everyone. You look nice every time I see you. You are kind. You are a good listener. You make me smile. You make me happy. I feel good when you come to our class.*

Wasn't it wonderful that the children found all these positive qualities in a dog? He's kind, a good listener, and nice to everyone, and he makes people happy. He sounds like a good friend to me. The kind of friend I would like to have. The kind of friend I would like to be.

God supplies us with many guidelines for how we should treat others. He asks us to love our neighbors and to treat others the way we want to be treated. He uses words such as *forgive* and *encourage* and *honor*. When I listen to God, I know everything I need to know about being a good friend. And when I observe my dog, I also learn, because surely God created the loving heart in Ernest that sets such a fine example.

Peggy Frezon

God, teach me the kind of unconditional love that a dog shows to others.

By Faith, Not Sight

Trust in the L<small>ORD</small> with all your heart and lean not on your own understanding; in all your ways submit to him, and he will make your paths straight.
—PROVERBS 3:5-6 (NIV)

As a pet sitter, I was blessed to care for all shapes, sizes, and breeds of pets. They all wrapped around my heart in unique ways. And one, a shivering Chihuahua that was going blind, held a special place in my being.

When Louie met me, he began biting at my ankles. He couldn't see this new stranger, but he needed to defend his home. I learned early on that UGG boots were great for meeting new dogs, especially Chihuahuas that liked to nibble ankles. Nothing could bite through those.

Each visit, I had a specific and involved procedure for eye drops and meds that needed to be given to Louie. I had to hold him so he wouldn't hide from me between my giving him his different eye drops. This cuddle-and-med session took about thirty minutes, and it became so special. Both Louie and I looked forward to the sessions. In between drops, he would nuzzle my neck and give kisses. Sometimes he would get so comfortable, he would fall asleep.

Though he couldn't see me, he trusted this stranger who came in twice a day to care for him and to keep him away from danger when he was outside. On his own, he might have ended up down the street at another house, but leaning on me, he got everything he wanted and love to boot.

If I trusted God as surely as a blind Chihuahua trusted me, how different would my path be? Not just dependence on God, but radical dependence, as if I were sightless, is where real trust begins.

Devon O'Day

God, please be my vision. When my trust falters, strengthen it for me. Amen.

How Big Is Your God?

He upholds the universe by the word of his power.
—HEBREWS 1:3 (ESV)

"May I pet your dog?"

The question was a common one when I took our Leonberger, Lancelot, out in public. Eventually growing to more than 130 pounds with the height to match, he was a gorgeous tan, black, and rust-colored dog that stopped people in their tracks with his looks and size.

But Lancelot would also stop in his tracks when he saw strangers. Once a puppy that adored new people, our dog became fearful as he grew, eventually requiring us to work with a professional trainer to reduce his paranoia to a livable level.

Never aggressive, my giant-breed dog would simply try to flee if strangers reached to pet him. My job when taking him out in public was to protect him from such well-meaning advances. I told the man on this occasion that my dog was too fearful for him to pet.

He looked at my Leonberger and shook his head. "Doesn't he know how big he is?"

It seems accurate to assume such a large dog wouldn't have reason to be afraid. But I realized later that a similar question could be asked of me.

I'm often plagued by worry, and I'm downright terrified of danger. At such times, someone could ask me with the same incredulous tone, "Don't you know how big your God is?"

The truth is our God is bigger than we can imagine. He is bigger than anything we fear. He is big enough to uphold the universe with a word of His power.

He is big enough to keep us safe in His loving care forever.

Jerusha Agen

Lord, help me to remember You are bigger and more powerful than even the worst things I face. Help me to trust in Your promise to always provide refuge in Your everlasting arms. In Jesus's name. Amen.

Press On

Brethren, I do not count myself to have apprehended; but one thing I do, forgetting those things which are behind and reaching forward to those things which are ahead, I press toward the goal for the prize of the upward call of God in Christ Jesus.
—PHILIPPIANS 3:13-14 (NKJV)

Every week, spunky Hettie conquers another exploit. She is the most adorable two-pound Boston terrier we have ever seen. She seems convinced she is a stunt puppy, jumping and running and taking risks like a fearless daredevil.

You can see determination in her eyes. They also tattle on her when she's about to do something audacious. A teeny little creature, she faced off with two recliners, jumping from one opened recliner to another—with a good amount of space between. She negotiated the odd angle she needed to navigate her jump.

The first jump ended in a fail. She plopped to the ground rather than hitting her mark. She shook it off, from shaking head to wiggly tail. Then she started all over again. The second jump missed the goal but came closer. I lost track of how many jumps she attempted. Each time, Hettie's stubborn determination motivated her to try again.

You can imagine our elation when she made it.

Watching her has inspired me. I pray that I will have Hettie's ability to not be distracted by my past failures and press on toward the goal until I fulfill the challenge. I remind myself not to let the times I miss the mark rob me of my vision to succeed. I want the outcome of following Jesus to motivate me more than the worry of getting it wrong. With dogged determination, despite multiple attempts, with God's help I will achieve daunting tasks.

Kathy Carlton Willis

***Remind me, Lord, that with dogged determination
I can achieve tasks that seem daunting at first.***

A Pint-Size Protector

***The angel of the LORD encamps around those
who fear him, and he delivers them.***
—PSALM 34:7 (NIV)

My friend Julie's Chihuahua-papillon mix, Finn, has earned the nickname "Ten Pounds of Crazy," even though he might weigh even less than that. Though sweet and playful, he came to her without training, so she had to work with him a lot, especially on not growling at random people and dogs that are five times his size.

One afternoon, Julie and I had Finn with us when we went out for coffee, so we chose a table outside, and Julie kept him on her lap. Finn was surprisingly calm, until a man said hello to us in passing. Then Finn started growling. Thinking he was up to his usual antics, Julie corrected Finn and apologized to the man. When the man stopped to talk to us on the way back to his car, Finn growled even more. Again, Julie shushed him and apologized.

As soon as the man was gone, Julie whispered, "Wow, Finn really didn't like that guy." Both being writers, we exchanged wild ideas about what Finn sensed in that suspicious person. After a while, though, we stopped making up stories and considered the possibility that Finn really had been protecting us.

At the time, I was working through painful memories of being lured in by a predator. Though it hurt to recall how many red flags I had missed, I could also see how God protected me from a much worse scenario. The signs I had ignored could now be lessons on what to pay attention to in the future. Finn's growl became a reminder of God's protective warnings as I learn to trust Him to keep me safe.

Jeanette Hanscome

God, thank You for the times You've protected me from harm, and the experiences that have given me wisdom for the future.

An Unlikely Servant

When the angel of the LORD appeared to Gideon, he said, "The LORD is with you, mighty warrior."
—JUDGES 6:12 (NIV)

Before we started service-dog training, the owner of Tails for Life, Jake, warned us that 90 percent of mixed breeds failed to complete the program. Unpredictable temperament and unknown breed characteristics hindered their success as service dogs. Would Callie's excess energy and stubborn tendency to follow her nose be her downfall? Could my fifty-pound border collie / hound mix, a kill-shelter rescue, compete with the purebred canines in her class?

As we prepared for a field-trip test to determine if Callie would continue the program, I doubted her. Upon entering the department store and approaching the escalators, most of the dogs walked onto the moving staircase as if they'd been born for the task. I considered their lineages of service as we neared the front of the line. Jake reminded me that my love for Callie, our established trust, and my confident presence would help her serve me. "She wants to please you," he said. "Walk with confidence. She'll follow your lead."

I took a deep breath and exhaled a prayer as I stepped onto the escalator. Callie walked by my side and stood next to me, tail wagging, until we stepped off. The group cheered.

Callie the Service Dog now serves me—her master—wherever God sends us. Why did I doubt her?

Well, I doubt myself and God's ability to use me when I focus on my limited capabilities and flawed character. Like Gideon—once called "mighty warrior" by an angel who assured him of God's constant presence—I'm tempted to test God before stepping out in obedience and faith. Believing what God says about me and trusting that He is always with me, I can walk with Spirit-empowered confidence and courage . . . even when I feel like I'm the most unlikely servant.

Xochitl Dixon

On the days when I feel unworthy, Lord, and I don't trust myself to serve You well, remind me to walk with confidence.

What the Pigs Are Having

Do not fret because of evildoers, nor be envious of the workers of iniquity.
—PSALM 37:1 (NKJV)

Mojo stared at the pigs. He knew not to approach the electric fence, but he was as close as he could get without feeling the shock. His tongue hung out, and the look in his eyes was mesmerized longing. On the other side of the fence, my daughter's two pigs devoured the table scraps she had tossed over to fatten them.

Mojo is her beloved rescue dog (and one of my favorite dogs in the world). He lives inside her house. He sleeps on or beside Hannah's bed. He's pampered, petted, and provided the best dog food and treats available.

The pigs aren't even given names because soon they will meet their intended fate. They sleep in a wooden shelter outdoors and aren't free to roam the yard the way Mojo does. They rummage in the ground, eat their swill, and enjoy the occasional gift of scraps. But Mojo envied their lot.

For the first time, I understood how ridiculous it looks to God when I envy the pleasures enjoyed by those outside His family. But even from my secure place inside God's family, I occasionally envy them the worldly feast in which they indulge.

God showed me my own heart as I watched Mojo, and I felt a new level of humility impress my spirit. I belong to the very family of God and have a place at His table. Whatever makes me sometimes long for more?

Lori Stanley Roeleveld

When I feel tempted to envy the worldly pleasures enjoyed by others, remind me that I reside in Your house, God.

God's Pomeranian Plan

*"For as the heavens are higher than the earth,
so are My ways higher than your ways,
and My thoughts than your thoughts."*
—ISAIAH 55:9 (NKJV)

It was the first day of the new year, and I was feeling out of shape. "This year, I am going to start walking at the mall every morning," I pledged, "no matter what."

Later the same day, my neighbor Jean called. "Would you mind feeding and walking Amy, my little Pomeranian, every morning and afternoon for one week?"

"My pleasure" was my reply.

The first morning of my walking duties was bitter cold. I regretted telling Jean "my pleasure." The truth was, no matter how much I love animals, it would still be "my inconvenience."

When I arrived at Amy's house, a fluffy, dancing ball of orange fur with sparkly polished-stone brown eyes greeted me. She finished her hello by licking my leg, leaving a trail of dripping doggy drool. I pulled back.

Then I took another look—and came face to face with the earnest gaze of a Pomeranian, inviting me to be her friend. As an exclamation point, she made sure to slurp my pant leg again.

The two of us headed outside into the frigid morning. The more we walked, the more I felt a warmth coming from my little companion—from her little Pom heart to mine. Back at the house, after her meal and water, she curled into a ball, using my foot as her pillow, and fell asleep. I closed my eyes for a bit . . . revived in a way that a walk at the mall could never make me feel.

My early mornings with Amy were not an unpleasant chore at all. They were a New Year's gift from God, whose mysterious ways brought me an adorable Pom filled with love.

Sandra Clifton

Lord, whenever I'm tempted to complain about inconveniences, help me be open to the joy I might find.

Rejoicing Always

"Why do you see the speck that is in your brother's eye, but do not notice the log that is in your own eye?"
—MATTHEW 7:3 (ESV)

I said I wasn't going to do it again—fall for one of the oldest fallacies of humankind. After having many puppies, the last one harder to raise than all those before, I had decided I would never get another puppy. I didn't handle puppy-rearing well. Sleepless nights and the need to constantly supervise a destructive ball of unceasing energy were not good for my psychological health.

But like so many people before me, my resolve gradually weakened under the persistent thoughts about how cute puppies are, the comfort they can be, and the wonderful adult dog that would be my friend when puppyhood was over.

The puppy who broke me down was Galen, a chunky, fluffy, brown-and-black Leonberger who was too adorable to believe. He was also a terror in the early days. I reached the end of my rope a few days after I brought him home, at which point I was already in the talk-to-the-puppy-who-doesn't-understand phase. On that particularly frustrating day, I said to Galen, "I wouldn't be having such a hard time if you would stop behaving so badly!"

He didn't even look up from trying to destroy a nearby box. But as soon as the words left my lips, they seemed to echo back, aimed at me. I was the one who was behaving badly. My attitude had been sour all day. I was short-tempered and unloving with the puppy and my family members. Sure, I was exhausted and stressed. But that was no excuse. After all, I'm called to rejoice in all circumstances and demonstrate the love of Christ to others, even when I'm tired. I guess the speck that I needed—to help me see the log in my own eye—was a puppy named Galen.

Jerusha Agen

When someone bothers me, or when I'm having a bad day, help me stop before I react and take an honest look at myself.

Dogs do speak, but only to those who know how to listen.

ORHAN PAMUK, AUTHOR

The Prayer Solution

***The Lord will watch over your coming
and going both now and forevermore.***
—PSALM 121:8 (NIV)

It was the dead of winter in the Berkshires when I first noticed the signs: two missing pugs, their pictures side by side.

Posters for lost pets upset me. A picture makes it worse. An image infiltrates my mind of the poor frightened creature trying to find home. I think of how panic-stricken my wife, Julee, and I would be if our golden Gracie was missing. Just imagining Gracie lost makes my heart race. *Maybe I should never let her off leash. Maybe I should never let her out of my sight!*

I mentioned the missing dogs to my vet not long after. She said an ASPCA survey she'd read verified that more than 90 percent of lost dogs are found and nearly as great a percentage of lost cats. That surprised me. My assumption had been far more pessimistic.

So I asked an editor at our animal devotional magazine about lost pets. She reminded me we did an advice column on it once.

"Posters are great," she said. "They really work. Social media, too. Instagram, Facebook. That's why you should always have a good, clear picture of your pet."

I rushed home and took a mug shot of Gracie. Several angles. "I'm surprised there's room on your phone for another picture of her," Julee said, laughing, so I explained. "Maybe," she said, "you should just say a prayer for the pugs and their owner and not get so freaked out."

It was the solution I should have seen for myself, but as so often happens, my self-centered fears blinded me. What other problems in the world should I be praying for instead of turning from? I can think of a few.

Edward Grinnan

Lord, help me believe in Your protection rather than believing my fears. I know You watch over me. Please watch over the lost ones.

Well Done!

"His master replied, 'Well done, good and faithful servant! You have been faithful with a few things; I will put you in charge of many things. Come and share your master's happiness!'"
—MATTHEW 25:21 (NIV)

I leaned over and patted my two-year-old golden retriever, Petey. "Goood booooy," I said, drawing out the *o*'s. I say this often. It makes us both happy. My preschool granddaughters even copy my intonation when they say, "Goood boooy."

Recently, people posted photos on Facebook of their dogs, just before and just after being called "Good boy." Big dogs, little dogs, fluffy dogs, all manner of dogs, each posing for the camera. In the before photos, the dogs' ears are flat, their heads down, and they often looked disengaged. But after the words of praise, their ears are perked, their chins are lifted, and their eyes are wide. And best of all, they actually appear to be smiling. Clearly, the praise has a positive effect.

I wondered, what would it look like if there were photographs of us just before and after being told we had done a good job? I imagine that our expressions would change from those of boredom, apathy, or discouragement to those of joy. Our eyes would widen, furrowed brows would soften, and we would smile. Thinking about this makes me want to encourage others. Everyone loves to receive approval and praise.

Of course, there is no greater praise than what we will hear on the judgment day. Ultimately, how our faces will shine when one day we're told, "Well done, good and faithful servant."

Peggy Frezon

***Lord, I know that You see the work I do.
Help me remember to praise others, too.***

Every Trick in the Book

Search me, God, and know my heart; test me and know my anxious thoughts. See if there is any offensive way in me, and lead me in the way everlasting.
—PSALM 139:23-24 (NIV)

When I was in college, my family got a black cocker spaniel named Dancer. He was full grown but not too old to learn tricks, so we taught him to sit, lie down, play dead, roll over, shake hands, and high-five. Dancer quickly caught on that doing tricks got him treats, so he made a routine of giving me and my sisters pitiful looks when we were eating, hoping we'd say "Dancer, sit" and toss him something when he obeyed. If his sad eyes didn't move us, he would sit, then lie down, and then roll over. Sometimes he frantically went through his entire repertoire until my sisters and I cracked up and one of us tossed him a treat.

Dancer came to mind recently. While waiting impatiently for God to answer a request that I must admit was selfish, I had written a series of prayers in my journal, each one getting more desperate. I had tried everything: pouring out my heart, being specific in Jesus's name, finding a scripture that supported my noncritical need, and so on. When God finally came through, I composed a prayer of thanks. Then I remembered those other pages in my journal and wondered if I had come across like Dancer, trying every trick in the book until God gave me what I wanted.

My journals are filled with evidence of my tendency to beg instead of trusting that God heard me the first time and knows what's best for me. His kindness in granting even some of my frivolous desires testifies to His patience. Today, it also motivates me to try not to behave like a whimpering puppy so often.

Jeanette Hanscome

Heavenly Father, thank You for hearing me, whether my requests are important or self-centered. Help me to recognize the difference as I learn to trust You to know my needs. Amen.

Noise Control

*A gentle answer turns away wrath,
but a harsh word stirs up anger.*
—PROVERBS 15:1 (NIV)

There is a moment when you realize that your parenting techniques might not be working.

My boxer dog, Tyson, had begun to communicate with me by barking. At some point in his growing-up years, I allowed a bit of freedom and, boy, he grabbed it and ran. To be fair, I was raising a human baby at the same time he was a puppy. Babies get priority over puppy training, so Tyson became the crazy one.

That dog thinks bark-yelling at me will get him the attention he deserves. And just as a mother knows the different cries of her baby, I know the different barks of my dog.

Short, persistent barks? "Gotta go; gotta go."

Crazy, obnoxious barks accompanied by bouncing? "Good, you're home. Feed me now!"

Barking with a few low growls? "You told me no to a dog treat, and I don't like it. I will talk back to you, then move to *extremely* loud barking."

My husband's words to me when I arrive home and Tyson starts barking at me? "He didn't do this when you were gone." I give up. The harshness of consistent barking from Tyson makes me annoyed and angry, and if I yell at him, he runs away and hides.

If I respond to Tyson, or to those around me, with harsh words or respond sharply to an innocent question, I push them away. Instead, my responses should be in love. Gentleness is always the best answer. I want my words to draw others close.

Reaching for Tyson, I pull him in for a hug. He snuggles close. Maybe I didn't really know what that barking meant after all.

Twila Bennett

May these words of my mouth and this meditation of my heart be pleasing in Your sight, Lord, my Rock and my Redeemer.

Little Shadows

The righteous care for the needs of their animals.
—PROVERBS 12:10 (NIV)

My mother had an affinity for the smallest of dogs. I think she preferred a tiny breed that could sit with her on the sofa or be held in her arms.

Tina, a Chihuahua-mix pup, needed a home, and Mom welcomed her gladly. Tipping the scale at around two pounds as an adult dog, Tina reminded me of a tiny black stallion—elegant and slender, with shiny fur. She was so small, we had to be careful we didn't step on her. But her high-pitched bark made her presence known in our home until she died of old age.

One day, while jumping and playing in our backyard, where my siblings and neighbor kids gathered on summer days, Tina fell from a ledge and broke her skinny leg. My mother, who didn't drive, ran out to the yard and then managed to find a ride to the veterinarian.

I had seen a white plaster cast on a friend at school who had broken her arm; all of us in the classroom signed our names on it. But to see a similar plaster cast on a tiny dog's stick-like leg touched my heart. It represented to me the tender care of a human for a hurting animal.

Tina's three good legs somehow supported her broken leg as she trotted across the floor, with a resilience that made my heart melt. When someone said her name, she persevered to come for a loving pat. Soon her cast came off, and she was good as new.

Toy breeds are said to be their owner's "little shadows." I realize now how Mom must have loved her buddy at her feet, as busy as she was raising a large family.

After Tina died, other dogs joined our family. But for me, the tiniest one holds the most endearing memories in my heart.

Kathleen Ruckman

***Dear God, thank You for the "little shadows"
at our feet—those tiny blessings in fur
that follow us around to let us know
they need and love us too. Amen.***

In His Steps

Those who know your name trust in you, for you,
LORD, have never forsaken those who seek you.
—PSALM 9:10 (NIV)

Printz was an adorable ball of fluffy, brilliant white fur. As a pup, he resembled a polar bear cub with lively black eyes. A Japanese spitz, Printz proved typical of the breed: personable and easy to train. He was also trusting. I remember the first time we took Printz to Ishikawa Beach in Okinawa. When his little paws sank into the deep sand, he locked his legs and looked up at us uncertainly. We moved ahead of him, coaxing him to follow. Reassured, Printz took small prancing steps until he felt safe enough to break into a clumsy run.

As we moved closer to the waves, he hesitated again. The sand felt firmer, but wet—another new sensation. Again, Printz looked up, as if asking for permission to move forward. We reassured him again, but paid close attention, not wanting him to get swept away in the undertow.

Looking back on that family outing, I can clearly see how I should be more like Printz. As I face new situations in life, it is in my best interest to turn to my heavenly Father for guidance and reassurance. Just as we watched over Printz's puppy steps, the Lord watches over me, urging me forward when it's safe to take the next step. It's when I don't look to Scripture for guidance, when I don't pray for wisdom and insight, that I'm more likely to get swept away into difficulties. God loves me. He loves you too. He wants the best for us. We can trust Him completely.

Shirley Raye Redmond

God, when facing the unknown, help me remember that I can trust You with anything.

Lost Right Where I Left Her

Be still before the LORD and wait patiently for him.
—PSALM 37:7 (ESV)

I love to hike and always wanted a dog that would stay close in the woods around our home while having freedom to run and explore on its own. Bay, my small chocolate Lab, would do just that.

I trained Bay to heel, stay, lie down, stop, and come with both voice and hand signal commands. If anyone approached or I heard another animal, I wanted her to stop and stay even if she couldn't hear my voice. The training proved very important and probably saved her life on several occasions. We were as close as human and dog can be.

We had been hiking together for a few miles one day when it dawned on me that Bay wasn't nearby, and I hadn't seen her for several minutes. Even though we were in a wide-open national forest, it was unusual for us to break sight of each other. I immediately turned in my tracks and started searching.

I came upon a small rise, and there she was—sitting at attention and patiently waiting for me. Bay watched carefully for my command to come. Only then did I remember saying to her, "Sit, stay," while I listened to a birdcall. She was simply being trustingly, patiently, and lovingly obedient. How proud I was of her, and how embarrassed I was of me. I had forgotten my friend!

O Father, I prayed silently, *forgive me for not having the trust in You at times that Bay has in me.* He reminds me over and over in Scripture to trust in Him and wait patiently for Him. God has often revealed His love for me through this loyal, loving Labrador.

Randy Benedetto

Whether You give the order to stand still or to move forward, Lord, remind me to always be attentive to Your voice.

Second-Chance Dog

*The Lord is not slow in keeping his promise,
as some understand slowness. Instead he is
patient with you, not wanting anyone to perish,
but everyone to come to repentance.*
—2 PETER 3:9 (NIV)

I had been afraid of dogs since I was a small child. But when my daughter begged to adopt an eighty-five-pound mutt from a shelter, I gave in on one condition: Bandit would be my daughter's dog. Two weeks later, she moved away for college, and Bandit decided that *I* was his person.

He followed me everywhere—whining outside the bathroom door, trotting behind me as I worked in the kitchen, wedging himself between any visitor and me. Big and beefy, with a shiny black coat and white blaze, Bandit had been abused at some point. His tail had been hacked off, leaving him with a stub, and his muzzle was peppered with gray. He was a second-chance dog if ever there was one.

One rainy morning, I put the teakettle on the stove, then stepped backward, tripping over Bandit. "Quit following me!" I yelled. Bandit hung his head. I stomped into the bathroom to take a shower. Over the water's spray, I heard frantic barking. He couldn't be without me for five minutes? Maybe I would give him back—I didn't care much for dogs anyway. I wrapped myself in a towel and opened the door, wagging my forefinger. "Hush!" But he kept barking and running to the kitchen, until I followed.

On the stove, the teakettle glowed bright red, and smoke filled the kitchen. I switched off the burner, grabbed a mitt, and flung the kettle out the back door onto the wet grass. Bandit flinched when I reached for him—and my heart melted. I sank to my knees and buried my face in his fur, begging his forgiveness. As Bandit licked away my tears, I became a dog lover. Like our merciful God, he was willing to give me a second chance too.

Linda S. Clare

*Thank You for the second chances, God.
Don't let me forget to extend forgiveness
and compassion to others, too.*

Minnie's Sticky Situation

He lifted me out of the slimy pit, out of the mud and mire; he set my feet on a rock and gave me a firm place to stand.
—PSALM 40:2 (NIV)

One spring afternoon, I took my dog, Minnie, for a walk along the side of our house. We headed toward the back but stopped before we got to the field. The weeds were nearly as tall as my almost-six-pound Yorkie. Time to mow.

We had turned around to go inside when Minnie spotted a lizard. She chased it under the hammock and through the weeds. The lizard ran up a palm tree where it found freedom just beyond Minnie's reach.

Since Minnie hasn't learned to climb trees, I convinced her to continue her pursuit another day, and we went inside. I undid her leash at the entryway and walked to the kitchen. Minnie wouldn't budge. She sat on the rug and waited.

I turned back to see why Minnie wasn't at my feet. Little green teardrop-shaped prickly pods clung to her hair from the bottom of her chin to the tips of her toes.

They stuck to her like glue and didn't allow her much room to move.

But Minnie knew just what to do. She waited for me to rescue her. She reminded me that no matter the circumstance I find myself in, Jesus is always right there with me. He is my Rescuer.

I painstakingly combed through Minnie's hair to remove the prickly pods, but it took a shower to remove their sticky remnants.

I'm thankful God not only cleanses the sin from my life but also removes the sticky remnants from my heart. All I have to do is ask.

Crystal Storms

Lord, thank You for being my Rescuer. Your grace keeps my foot from slipping, and in You I have a firm place to stand. Amen.

Seek the Son

So that they should seek the Lord, in the hope that they might grope for Him and find Him, though He is not far from each one of us.
—ACTS 17:27 (NKJV)

I never knew dogs were natural heat seekers! At just fourteen weeks old, Mijo the Boston terrier taught me a valuable life lesson.

Mijo [*MEE-hoe]* learned what time of day the sun shone through our front door. Every day, like clockwork, he stopped whatever he was doing to get to his sunny spot. There he enjoyed leisurely naps wrapped in the warmth of the sunbeams.

One day, he spent the early hours playing outdoors. Suddenly, even though he was having a good time, he urgently wanted to go inside. Once I opened the door, he darted past me. Curious to see where he went, I followed him through the house. Wouldn't you know that Mijo had already found his place in the sun, and his snores sounded like a chainsaw!

By simply replacing the word *sun* with *Son*, I pondered several lessons. It is good to get in the habit of seeking the Son. The warmth of Jesus's embrace is all I need. I grow closer to Jesus when I seek the Son early and daily, like clockwork. I can develop this habit, just as Mijo did. It is second nature for him to look for the sun. Is it second nature for me to daily look for the Son?

Not only does the Son provide warm, welcoming intimacy, He also gives me rest when I come to Him. Mijo fell asleep right away when he hunkered down in the warmth of the sunbeams. I can find that same instant rest in Jesus. And not just physically, but emotionally, mentally, and spiritually as well. When I rest in Jesus, I can put all other thoughts to rest. No more doing or striving, just being—all found in the Son.

Kathy Carlton Willis

God, remind me each day to help me find my place in the Son.

A young dog's faith is absolute.... Dogs are notorious for hope. Dogs believe that this morning, this very morning, may begin a day of fascination, easily grander than any day in the past.

DONALD McCAIG, AUTHOR

Bravely Facing the Fog

When I am afraid, I put my trust in you. In God, whose word I praise, in God I trust; I shall not be afraid. What can flesh do to me?
—PSALM 56:3-4 (ESV)

It had been cold and snowy in the Berkshires until a sudden warm front rolled in that January night, shrouding the old hills in a thick, velvety fog. I let Gracie out after dinner for her evening reconnoiter. I was poking the fire in the woodstove when I heard her barking rather emphatically out in the yard. I looked out the window. There she stood in the mist, turning a slow circle and sounding off into the gloom. A deep, chesty bark, assertive but not aggressive, slightly muffled, the effort lifting her front paws a bit off the ground with each volley.

"What's got into her?" my wife, Julee, asked, joining me at the window.

"The fog," I said. "It messes with her night vision." Goldens have superb eyesight, even in the dark. But not tonight. She couldn't see past her own wet, black nose.

"Should I go get her?" I asked Julee.

"No, leave her. She's just doing her job."

What a thought! Gracie was barking out warnings to any would-be intruders who might infiltrate her yard under cover of fog, warding off threats, letting the hills know she was on duty, keeping us safe. What a brave dog!

I wondered if I was that brave—brave when it counted, brave in my faith. I like to believe my faith is clear and unwavering, and yet there are times when I can't see my way, when my spiritual visibility is compromised by the fog of fear or doubt or regret. It is at those moments that I must stand in the dark and proclaim my trust in that unseen heaven.

"Gracie is too brave to let a little fog bother her," Julee said. I would be brave, too, the next time a spiritual fog found me.

Edward Grinnan

When I grope and falter, when I fear and I doubt, lead me, Lord, through the gloom to Your eternal light.

Keeping Focus

Look to the L*ORD *and his strength; seek his face always.
—PSALM 105:4 (NIV)

My service dog, Callie, struggles with keeping her focus on me when surrounded by distractions. Our professional trainers at Tails for Life recommended I remove treats as a motivator when I want her to look at me. They wanted forward movement and pleasing me, not tasty snacks, to motivate Callie. They instructed me to stop periodically during walks, look down at Callie, and quietly wait for her to lift her eyes to meet mine. The moment she turned away from the distractions and locked into my gaze, I was supposed to praise her and say, "Yes! Let's go."

Our thirty-minute walks became hour-long strolls with extended stops as I waited for Callie to choose me—her silent and trying-to-be-patient master—over the distractions that screamed for her attention. With encouragement from our trainers, I've resisted the urge to bribe my dog as we continue practicing, and now Callie is improving in this skill, which is vital for a service dog. Though some days are harder than others, our Tails for Life family assures me that following me will eventually become Callie's greatest reward.

During one of our extended training walks, I cried out to God in frustration. *Lord, why won't she focus on me?*

That prayer pierced my heart. How often have I failed to focus on my loving Master—Jesus—when surrounded by distractions? As the world screams for my attention, my eyes and heart wander from God. But as I acknowledge His constant presence, praise Him, grow closer to Him, and share Him with others (see Psalm 105:1–3), my desire to follow Him increases.

God invites me to keep my eyes on Him, because He knows I'll need His strength and guidance (verse 4). As I trust God more, I'll want to stop, check in with Him, then go wherever He leads.

Xochitl Dixon

Good Shepherd, please help me check in with You before I move forward in every aspect of this life You've entrusted to me. Amen.

Trust in the Valley

*To you they cried out and were saved;
in you they trusted and not put to shame.*
—PSALM 22:5 (NIV)

Cancer. I had expected something minor, something treatable. Instead, I was told my beloved dog, Norway, had a cancer that would kill him in three to four months. He was only five years old—too young to die.

The diagnosis hit hard and painfully chipped at my heart, preparing it to shatter when the end would come, far sooner than I had expected. The apparent injustice of the diagnosis strangled me. Norway was healthy and happy. He should have had more years to enjoy life.

Fear clawed at the back of my grief. How would I face this? I couldn't watch him suffer, couldn't see him be destroyed by the disease that would take him from me. The pain felt too intense for me to bear.

But then the Holy Spirit prompted me to remember to trust God. Did I trust Him only with unimportant things? Or did I trust Him with what I loved most? Through tears, I handed my fears over.

Two years later, my sweet dog, Norway, was still with us, living his life to the fullest while we savored every moment we had with him. The cancer specialists were astounded. Some disbelieved that the impossible could have happened.

But I hold up this testimony as a witness, against my own doubts and the doubts of others, that I can trust in the steadfast love of God. He is the giver of good gifts who can and *will* bring about His plan. I can trust Him even with my precious ones.

Jerusha Agen

Father, I thank You that in the darkest times, I can trust You with the people and things dearest to me because You love me and are more than able to work all things for good. Amen.

No Better Friend

A friend loves at all times, and a brother is born for a time of adversity.
—PROVERBS 17:17 (NIV)

My niece Kacey loves to hike. Just out of college, she often kidded her family that she would like to abandon all career paths so that she was freed up to explore as many national parks as possible. Two years ago, she adopted five-month-old Smokey, an adorable black Lab puppy. He has become her constant companion as they explore the wilds of Utah, Nevada, and Arizona.

Kacey always makes sure to bring extra water for herself and her dog when they venture out into the unforgiving heat of the desert. One day, they departed for a planned six-mile round-trip hike. Their destination was the falls, and Smokey made it there just fine. He ran around, splashed, swam, and rested in the shade before it was time to begin the journey back home.

But Kacey could tell he was tired. He was sluggish, didn't want water (though he desperately needed it), and lay down and didn't want to get up. Fighting panic on behalf of her dog, Kacey picked up her sixty-five-pound friend and carried him a mile back to the trailhead. Each time she found a creek, she practically threw him into the water, sitting immersed with him to help him cool down. When they reached her car, Smokey seemed much better and slept in her lap most of the way back to town.

Kacey's loving care of Smokey reminded me of the friends I have who help lift me when I am exhausted or feel unable to carry on. There are people in my life I can count on if I am in need, if I want to go on an adventure, or if we just want to sit quietly in the backyard and enjoy the sunset together. The Lord has placed me in these relationships to teach me how to both give and receive love and encouragement.

Liz Kimmel

Help me be a supportive presence for all my loved ones, whether they walk on two legs or four.

Be the Person . . .

*"The L*ORD* your God is with you, the Mighty Warrior who saves. He will take great delight in you; in his love he will no longer rebuke you, but will rejoice over you with singing."*
—ZEPHANIAH 3:17 (NIV)

I received a wonderful gift for my birthday this year—a soft blue T-shirt, featuring an image of a retriever and the words *Be the person your dog thinks you are*. I love this message, perhaps because I often feel as though I'm undeserving of the love my dogs bestow upon me.

Last week, I had a less-than-stellar interaction with a family member, and I returned home brooding about how I could have handled the situation with more grace. As I sank into the sofa, my dog Ernest snuggled up next to me and looked at me with pure, unreserved love. Ernest already thought I was patient and kind.

Another morning, I was berating myself for having eaten too many sweets the day before. When I looked in the mirror, I saw someone overweight and unattractive. Yet when Petey padded up and looked at me, his smiling eyes and wagging tail demonstrated his love. My dog wasn't concerned about the spare tire around my middle.

What is it about my dogs that enables them to see me as so wonderful? The way God sees me. God knows that underneath the cracks and flaws, the extra pounds and wrinkles, I am still worthy of His love. After all, He created us in His image. To be sure, my dogs love me; yet, this love pales in comparison with God's immense adoration. His unconditional love is a gift I will always treasure.

Peggy Frezon

Dear God, Your love for me is without limits. It isn't based on my successes or limitations. Help me to accept Your grace and to extend that grace to myself when I feel I don't measure up. Amen.

But I *Like* Chicken

For what I want to do I do not do, but what I hate I do.
—ROMANS 7:15 (NIV)

Max is just a great big black dog with very few teeth and stinky, itchy ears. He used to have teeth, and he used to be smaller, but he has *always* had stinky, itchy ears. From the time he was old enough to have checkups, veterinarians have prescribed antibiotics and anti-yeast medicine, and I tried all sorts of natural and internet cures, but nothing helped my big old dog get relief. Max cried pitifully every time I cleaned out those ears.

Then one day, I was shopping for food and supplies in a smaller, more rural town. I asked if they had any remedies for stinky ears that I had not tried. And the young woman behind the counter said, "It's probably the chicken."

What? Isn't chicken always the preferred protein for all living creatures? Isn't it healthier? All the questions popped into my head. But as it turned out, many dogs have reactions to even high-end chicken kibble. So, I spent a little extra on salmon food, and the itching and stinkiness stopped almost immediately. No medicine.

No cleaning. His ears just healed. But despite the positive result, whenever I had chicken of any kind, Max would stare at me, begging. He would salivate or try to steal any chicken scraps from the garbage. He wouldn't give up because, though it was bad for him, he just loved chicken.

How many of us are like that? We insist on something we know will cause repercussions if we do it, yet we are drawn to it.

There is no understanding why the moth is drawn to the flame, but God has a way of showing us the flame and equipping us with the strength to resist it. The more we resist, the easier it gets to walk away.

Devon O'Day

God, it isn't easy to walk in the ways You have planned for me as I'm drawn to the flames of my past. But will You ease the pull it has on me? Amen.

Sweet Fellowship

My soul waits for the Lord more than watchmen for the morning, more than watchmen for the morning.
—PSALM 130:6 (ESV)

I just hate it, but I had to do it five days a week—leave my best friend, Bay, and go to work.

Every morning, we went through the same routine. As she sensed I was getting ready to go, she would get antsy for the dog biscuit she knew I would give her just before I walked out the door. She would gently take her favorite treat and prance away, returning immediately without the biscuit to see me off.

Each evening, I would come through the door and drop to my knees, and the party would begin! Jumping, romping, rolling, yelping—well, enough about me, Bay went crazy too!

Suddenly, as if a lightbulb clicked on in her head, she would stop, dash into another part of the house, and trot proudly back with the bone I had given her that morning. She saved her treat all day for my return and our happy reunion.

Now the fun part! Bay would lie down on the carpet with the bone between her paws, a twinkle in her eye and her head cocked sideways, and give a little growl. I would pretend that I wanted to eat her bone, but she would grab it in her teeth and jump a few feet away. Always on the third charade, she would gobble down her biscuit with great delight, and I would bury her in hugs and loving.

People could use as much patience as this dog. When I wonder where God is and feel that He's far away during my lonely times or trials, I remember He promised that He will never leave me or forsake me. He always comes to me, and then we share sweet fellowship together.

Randy Benedetto

Thank You, Lord, for all the moments of fellowship that I share with You. I am blessed to know that we will always be together.

Expect Kindness

May the God of hope fill you with all joy and peace as you trust in him, so that you may overflow with hope by the power of the Holy Spirit.
—ROMANS 15:13 (NIV)

Ten years ago, my husband and I rescued a cocker spaniel named Maddie. Little did we know at the time that she would become the most sociable member of our family. Maddie never met a person, dog, cat, or butterfly she didn't like. In fact, she will persistently pursue friendship with any person or living thing that seems ambivalent about her existence, as if it's obvious that knowing her would make their lives better. She isn't wrong about that part.

Maddie's favorite day of the year is an annual fundraiser for the Humane Society, where she gets to wear her pumpkin costume and meet other dogs and new people. As soon as she sees me pull out her costume, her tail begins wagging dramatically. She knows exactly where she's going. Every single year, Maddie makes a fan club full of people who think she's absolutely adorable. I can't help but agree with them.

The thing about Maddie is that she lives her life expecting good things, so she, in turn, *sees* good things. She expects other dogs to be friendly. She expects new people will want to play with her. And she nearly always wins them over.

I want to live my own life more like this. All too often, I meditate on my fears of what could go wrong in life, as if it's up to me, in my own strength, to keep these things from happening. But doing so limits my perspective so that my fears become *what* I see. On the contrary, if I, like Maddie, expect kindness, I will find kindness. If I seek beauty, I will find that too. The same holds true for restoration, redemption, hope, and generosity. I become, in this way, what I see. Maddie's joy spills over to everyone she meets—and she challenges me to see the joy already abounding in the world around me.

Ashley Clark

Lord, help me to always seek the beautiful things in life.

Zoey the Cat Herder

"I am the good shepherd; I know my sheep and my sheep know me."

—JOHN 10:14 (NIV)

My sister Sherry's house is a menagerie of cats and dogs. Recently, Sherry added a shorthair Australian shepherd named Zoey. She hasn't had any formal dog training yet, but her natural herding instincts have come through in her interactions with the other pets—specifically, her routine of herding the cats, Luna and Cosmo, from the yard when Sherry wants them to come in for the night.

All Sherry has to do is open the door to the area where the cats hang out and say, "Zoey, go get Luna and Cosmo," and Zoey runs out, nudges one cat and then the other, then coaxes them across the yard and into the house. The image of Zoey herding cats is fascinating enough on its own, but what strikes me even more is that Luna and Cosmo let her do it. Recently, when I was at Sherry's house, Zoey tried to herd me up the stairs, and I gently shooed her away. But Luna and Cosmo, though they hesitate occasionally, know that Zoey is the one who ushers them inside before the coyotes and owls come out. They've grown to trust her as a friend who looks out for them.

Today, after a moment with Zoey, I considered my journey of learning to trust God's divine herding techniques in my life and with those I love. It has included many moments of resistance. But the more I get to know Him and watch His plans unfold, the more quickly I recognize nudges that urge me from my favorite resting places at His loving direction, either out of harm's way or to an exciting new purpose.

Jeanette Hanscome

Heavenly Father, thank You for looking out for me and those I love. Fill my memory with reminders of times You moved me for a good reason, so when I am tempted to resist a change, I will trust You enough to go where You want me. Thank You for being such a kind shepherd. Amen.

Annie's Favorite

LORD my God, I called to you for help, and you healed me.
—PSALM 30:2 (NIV)

After major shoulder surgery, I contacted a physical therapist. I wasn't exactly looking forward to the weekly appointments—a friend had warned that painful exercises with colorful stretchy bands awaited me. I grumbled going into my first PT session but was greeted by the therapist's assistant: a beautiful golden retriever named Annie.

Despite my lingering shoulder pain and stiffness, Annie the Greeter Dog instantly put me at ease. I stroked her soft, reddish-gold fur, gazed into her deep brown eyes, and could almost feel my blood pressure lowering. Then my therapist led me down a hallway, and Annie followed, plopping down in the treatment room's corner as I lay back on a padded table.

Annie slept when the therapist demonstrated helpful shoulder exercises I should do. But whenever I stretched my shoulder farther or tried a painful maneuver, Annie jumped up and poked her wet nose into my palm, as if trying to comfort me. Week by week, Annie and I got to know each other. I learned her favorite spot to scratch for a belly rub, and she learned which exercises gave me the most trouble. After a couple of months, I had made significant progress and worked those stretchy bands harder, just for her. I was sure I was Annie's favorite patient.

When I told the therapist, she smiled. "All my patients think Annie loves them best." I was crestfallen, until I thought back to that first appointment, when I was in near-constant pain and my arm was as stiff as a toy soldier's. Because of Annie's encouragement, my shoulder movement was getting better all the time and I was much stronger. Modern medicine cures many things and physical therapy is vital to the recovery process. Still, I wouldn't trade Annie's gentle nature and wet-nosed support for all the stretchy bands in the world.

Annie's encouragement (even if I really wasn't her favorite) reminded me that I can do the same thing: bring healing and help to others I encounter, through uplifting words and kind actions, every day.

Linda S. Clare

Dear Lord, may I follow Annie's shining example of encouragement to everyone You bring to me today. Amen.

The good Lord in his infinite wisdom gave us three things to make life bearable—hope, jokes, and dogs.

ROBYN DAVIDSON, AUTHOR

Reaching Out

***Do nothing from selfish ambition or conceit, but in
humility count others more significant than yourselves.***
—PHILIPPIANS 2:3 (ESV)

New York City dog runs are microcosms of the human population. You see friendly dogs and standoffish dogs, and the owners fall along the same divide. I'm somewhere in the middle. But not Gracie. As soon as we arrive at the dog run, Gracie immediately scouts for friends.

This morning she spotted a group trying to convince a Boston terrier named Barney to relinquish a tennis ball he had adamantly clamped down on. She joined them, her feathery tail swishing the air. It was quite a standoff, with the dogs in a semicircle in front of Barney, who was down on his haunches. Then all at once, he shot up, and the chase was on. Barney didn't get far before losing the ball. He skidded to a stop, but it was too late—a Lab had snatched it up. Soon it lost interest in the ball and abandoned it. Eventually, Gracie sauntered over and picked it up.

What she did next was remarkable: She trotted over to a man I recognized, who was sitting on a bench, reading the paper, his dog in his lap. The man usually kept to himself. So did his dog.

Politely as ever, and cautiously, Gracie approached. She dropped the ball at their feet, then sat. Another little standoff. Finally, the man lowered his *New York Times* and regarded Gracie. Then he smiled, picked up the ball, and gave it a little toss. Gracie bounded after it but ended up detouring to the entrance to check out a new canine arrival.

The man went back to his paper. His dog yawned and shifted in his lap. Gracie had greeted a new friend. She had done her good deed for the day. Had I?

Edward Grinnan

Lord, let me be more like Gracie and never hesitate to make a stranger a friend.

Bring on the Chute!

I sought the L<small>ORD</small>, and He heard me, and delivered me from all my fears.
—PSALM 34:4 (NKJV)

"Don't be surprised if he balks at first. Most dogs do." My mom issued the warning on the first day of puppy classes.

For the first two weeks, I held Kenai's leash, walked him around, and stopped at various signs. "Put dog in sit. Count to ten, release." Kenai obeyed every command.

The following week, agility stations sat in the yard, including a seesaw and a tire to jump through. Again, Mom warned, "He might be afraid. Just get him used to them this week."

Not my dog. He looked at the seesaw, walked up one side, hesitated when it wobbled, then trotted down the other side. On to the tire jump. I dropped his leash, walked to the other side, and called. He sailed through the tire in the first try. Even when the tire was raised to its fullest height, Kenai flew through the hole.

Last: the chute. Even some older dogs balked when seeing the tube of canvas. Not Kenai. He ran through, turned around, and went back the other way. Stunned, Mom showed me a shorter tunnel ending in a collapsed chute of canvas. She felt sure this would stump him. But Kenai ran into the tunnel section and streaked right through the folded material. No hesitation, no fears.

How would I handle a tunnel and a collapsed chute? I'd yank my leash from my owner and run. Fear of new things paralyzes me. But Jesus leads me to that tunnel, holds open the chute, and beckons me. If I kept my eyes on Him and not the surroundings, could I do it? One step . . . a second . . . then I'm coming out the other side. Safe, just as He promised.

Cathy Mayfield

The Bible says "fear not" 366 times in various ways—one for every day of the year, including leap year. So today, Lord—I won't be afraid, knowing You are there.

Mister and Mrs. Pomeranian

A man who has friends must himself be friendly, but there is a friend who sticks closer than a brother.
—PROVERBS 18:24 (NKJV)

Moving can be challenging even for the most extroverted person. As a borderline introvert, I found no appeal in the prospect of another new city. But a major promotion beckoned, and I couldn't turn it down. To make matters worse, my sister found herself in need of a long-term dog-sitter at the same time, due to a change in career. So Mister and Mrs. Pomeranian had to come with me.

Mister, a black miniature, stands only a foot off the ground. His long, straight hair bounces as he walks, just like that of his caramel-colored mate. Mrs. P. bounces along several inches taller than Mister. She usually sports a better attitude than her mate and can out-eat him any day of the week. Both enjoy walks, getting petted, lying on the couch, and yapping excitedly at the mailman.

My first apartment in Oklahoma City included a freestanding island that served as the Pomeranian dog track. Once ignited by something outside or on television,

Mister and Mrs. P. raced around the island, chasing each other and barking. I worried I might be evicted if the dogs refused to settle down. Fortunately, their outbursts lasted only a minute or so, and then they returned to the couch beside me or on my lap.

Oklahoma enjoys much warmer weather than I was used to in Chicago and is known for its strong thunderstorms that roll across the prairie. Mister and Mrs. P. abhor thunderstorms. Mister began barking at the first clap of thunder and kept growling until I petted his fur and reassured him with kind words.

How lonely my new city would have seemed without the gift of those visiting dogs. By the time my sister was ready to take them back, I had met several friends and even joined a tennis league. And God reminded me that Jesus is the Friend who sticks closer than a Pomeranian in a thunderstorm.

David L. Winters

***Thank You, God, for the little comforters
who help us navigate a new home.***

My Canine Caregiver

"Martha, Martha," the Lord answered, "you are worried and upset about many things, but few things are needed—or indeed only one. Mary has chosen what is better, and it will not be taken away from her."

—LUKE 10:41–42 (NIV)

It's not easy being a long-distance caregiver for my senior mother with mobility and vision issues. She lives alone, although she does have services in place to help: a visiting nurse, Meals on Wheels, and a Life Alert button. But I have one more secret tool that makes a great difference in her care.

I visit Mom as often as possible. On a recent visit, I sat at the kitchen table making a list, wondering if I had addressed every issue that needed attention. *God, help me to help Mom in the best way I can.* I looked over her bottles of pills. Was she taking her medication? I opened her refrigerator. Had she been eating properly? Was there a doctor appointment that needed scheduling?

But while I was taking care of all these details, my golden retriever, Ernest, was thinking about only one thing. He was up on the sofa, draped over my mom's lap, gazing up at her adoringly. He hadn't moved from her side since we had arrived.

It reminded me of the story of Martha and Mary. While Martha hurried to make all the preparations for Jesus, her sister Mary simply sat at his feet, listening attentively. Maybe I needed to take a lesson from Mary—and from Ernest.

I set down the pen and paper, walked over, and sat beside them on the couch. I'm not saying that certain details don't need to be attended to. But Ernest knows what's often needed most. Yes, Ernest is my secret tool. He provides the best TLC—and the finest example—anyone could ever give.

Peggy Frezon

Lord, show me how to fulfill the needs of those who could use a little extra attention.

The Best Way to Make a Bed

We love because he first loved us.
—1 JOHN 4:19 (NIV)

When my mother made up a bed, she made perfect hospital corners. She tried hard to teach me how to make a bed so tightly that I could bounce a quarter on it. I can make the bed smooth, but I'm still trying to master hospital corners.

It's even more challenging now because our little black-and-white spaniel, Rocky, thinks the big bed is his. He graciously lets us sleep with him. When we get up in the morning, I throw back the covers, shake them, and pull them tight. Ears flapping, Rocky jumps up into the middle of the bed and rolls around. He tosses the pillows with his freckled muzzle and burrows under the quilt until just the white tip of his tail peeks out. It's hard to get the bed anywhere near smooth.

One morning, in a hurry to get on with the day, I lost patience and yanked at the covers. "Rocky," I said, "my mother would never approve of the way you make the bed!"

The thought of my mother made me stop rushing, and I sat on the bed patting Rocky. I remembered that before we made the bed, my mother used to throw the covers over my head and tickle me until I couldn't stop laughing. I had been so focused on making perfect hospital corners, I had forgotten all the love behind her lessons.

Remembering the details of those happy mornings, I realized that God loves me the same way. Yes, He wants me to learn and grow, but He doesn't expect perfection. There is much joy to discover in His lessons.

Now when Rocky and I make up the bed, I fold the covers over him, and he rolls around. I build a fort of pillows, and he knocks it down. It's not the most efficient way to make up a bed, but it reminds me that I am so deeply loved that it doesn't matter if I can't make a hospital corner.

Lucy H. Chambers

Help me remember that the best way to do any chore is with love.

Eyes on the Prize

I press on toward the goal for the prize of the upward call of God in Christ Jesus.
—PHILIPPIANS 3:14 (ESV)

Sharing life with a Great Pyrenees taught me a lot about independent thinking. From his puppy years on, Magnus thought he knew best, and that made training a challenge.

When I tried to teach him the simple trick of "shake," asking him to put his paw in my hand, he acted for weeks like he had no idea what I wanted him to do. I knew he was smart enough, however, that he could have learned the trick within a couple of days.

I caught on that he wanted me to pick up his paw myself and give him a treat for doing nothing. When I started to require him to put his paw in my hand, he wasn't happy and resisted doing the trick.

But then I learned he would obey if he could see I held a treat, ready to reward him once he did what I asked. Unlike other eager-to-please dogs, Magnus was in this for the prize—the tasty treat. If I didn't have a treat in front of him, then giving me his paw wasn't worth it.

I had a hard time admitting what I eventually realized: I'm not all that different from Magnus. This Christian life can be hard. Trials and persecutions make me wonder if the effort to live in obedience to God is worth it. But then I read Bible passages that remind me why following Christ is infinitely worthwhile. Jesus is holding out a prize to me that's far better than any dog treat. He's given me an upward call to a joyful eternity with my Savior, where life will be greater than I can ever imagine. If I keep my eyes on His prize, I'll be able to press on today and for the rest of my days.

Jerusha Agen

Lord, help me keep my eyes on Your prize and not hesitate when I hear Your call.

Wonder Bread

But when you pray, go into your room, close the door, and pray to your Father, who is unseen. Then your Father, who sees what is done in secret, will reward you.
—MATTHEW 6:6 (NIV)

McKenzie, our boxer dog, was never one to be contained. We nicknamed her Houdini because she escaped any locked kennel by pounding on the door until the latch loosened. That wild girl would find the oddest items to destroy if left unattended. A doll from my childhood, my husband's socks, and bread. She absolutely adored bread due to taking it with her daily meds.

My husband and I arrived home one day to find McKenzie out of her crate again. She acted guilty, but it took a minute to figure out what else she had done. Then I discovered an empty plastic bread wrapper on the floor. The brand-new loaf had magically evaporated. Even the twist tie was still fastened, with not a crumb left inside.

Looking at McKenzie, I asked if she had eaten the bread. She quickly slunk back into the other room. My husband and I looked at each other incredulously and, at the same time, exclaimed, "How did she eat that whole loaf?" Video evidence probably would have shown her seventy-pound body flinging onto the counter, grabbing the loaf, and carefully pulling those slices, one by one, through the small hole she made in the wrapper. I still laugh at the intricate maneuvering it must have taken for her to reach her goal.

My Father calls me to pray with this same diligence. He promises that prayers lifted quietly will be answered and honored. And praying in secret communion brings my spiritual life to another level too. Believing in the power of prayer means getting on my knees and not just simply talking about it. And as McKenzie received a wonderful reward for her tenacity and dedication, so will I.

Twila Bennett

You tell me to go into my room, close the door, and pray. It seems so simple, but it is hard. Lord, help me to create this rhythm in my life. Amen.

Ralph's Transformation

Who redeems your life from destruction, who crowns you with lovingkindness and tender mercies.
—PSALM 103:4 (NKJV)

Ralph? I did a double take when I saw the young male cashier at the garden shop. I usually tried to avoid the man. He was always ill-mannered as he impatiently pushed my garden tools and plants down the conveyor belt and rustled customers through his line. In response to his rudeness, I internally grumbled and muttered under my breath throughout our transaction interaction. I inevitably marched out of the store, feeling like Mrs. Grump. Rude Ralph, I must confess, had that effect on me.

I approached Ralph, expecting to find Mr. Hyde. To my utter shock and amazement, I was face to face with Dr. Jekyll instead—earnest, polite, and on a mission to serve me. *What happened to Mr. Hyde?* My shoulders had been braced for battle, but now there was no reason.

It was Ralph, all right, but it was a brand-new Ralph, comfortable, with a generous smile. Whoa! I couldn't figure out the change.

As I picked up today's purchase of tools and small pots of flowers, a dash of movement caught my eye. Sticking out from Ralph's station was a dog, a Chihuahua mix, whose tail was thumping happily. "Who is that?" I asked.

"He's my dog!" Ralph announced proudly. "Found him outside my door last week." Nearby were bowls of water and food. Ralph smiled as he bent down to give his new friend a treat. Ralph seemed happy to be caring for the workmate curled at his feet.

I crossed to the exit, not grumbling or complaining but smiling. I waved goodbye to a grinning Ralph and the tail-wagging source of his newfound kindness. Perhaps if more dogs, like Ralph's much-loved friend, went to work with their owners, there would be fewer Hydes and more Jekylls.

And certainly fewer Mrs. Grumps.

Sandra Clifton

Lord, thank You for the company of dogs, whose kind and unselfish ways can change any atmosphere. Amen.

Jailbirds

***You were bought at a price. Therefore honor
God with your bodies.***
—1 CORINTHIANS 6:20 (NIV)

When my two escape-artist dogs got out of the fence and took off while I was at work, they were picked up by the county animal control. They both had tags and collars and were microchipped, but they would be spending the night in dog jail until I could pick them up the next morning.

At first, all I could do was be grateful they were safe and had not gotten picked up by a stranger or hit by a car. Then I worried they would have to spend the night in a cell. After all the money spent on fencing, premium beds, and food I cooked for them every night, they still took off into a world of danger, leaving safety and love in their rear view.

The next day, I paid their bail. And even though it was apparent I had done everything I could to contain them, I was penalized for letting my dogs run free. They came out as the animal control officer commented how obedient and well cared for they were. Tails wagging and joyful, they hopped in the back seat as if they'd had a glorious adventure. They never realized the danger they had escaped or that someone had paid the price for their safety. They didn't realize they had caused any problem at all.

We do this too. We break from the safety of home, family, church, good health choices, or any choice that serves our best and highest interests. Then, when someone has our back and God covers us in protection, we return as if nothing happened, happily blind to all the ways we have been covered and blessed. Even when we do not realize how precious we are to God, He loves us through our adventures and constantly wants to give us a way back to His arms.

Devon O'Day

God, thank You for always loving me and bringing me back to You. Amen.

Always Working

***Let us hold unswervingly to the hope we profess,
for he who promised is faithful.***
—HEBREWS 10:23 (NIV)

I smiled when the couple looked at my border collie mix, Callie, as we followed my husband into the restaurant. "That doesn't look like a service dog," said the woman with a scowl.

My joy faded, but Callie remained oblivious to the criticism. She walked confidently by my side as we followed the hostess. Once she seated us, I gave Callie the command to rest at my feet under the table. We enjoyed a wonderful dinner and a visit from the restaurant's manager. She handed us our bill and thanked us for choosing her restaurant before moving to the next table to visit with the patrons.

When I rose from my chair, Callie came from under the table and sat by my side. The manager turned toward us. "I had no idea you had a service dog with you."

"That's the point," I said with a grin. "She's always working, even when you don't see her."

God has taught me so much through my relationship with Callie. I see how she responds to my commands out of love, and I want to obey my Master—Jesus—with the same willingness and joy. I notice how Callie draws near to me when she's unsure about a situation, and I want to stay close to my Master, who promises He will care for me in all circumstances. But that night, when I explained how Callie was always working, God reminded me to be confident in His promises to work through what often seems like endless waiting seasons.

Xochitl E. Dixon

God, thank You for showing me how you are always with me, always in control, and always working— even when I don't see You.

> Dogs are not our whole life, but they make our lives whole.

ROGER CARAS, WRITER

To Know We're There

Are not two sparrows sold for a penny? Yet not one of them will fall to the ground outside your Father's care.
—MATTHEW 10:29 (NIV)

Julee called to say that something was wrong with Gracie. I rushed home, praying Gracie would greet me with her usual exuberance. Instead, she moved tentatively, leaned into my leg, and looked up at me imploringly. She was in pain.

Julee said our vet thought Gracie might have strained a muscle. "She prescribed pain pills and said to watch her for a few days." Julee's eyes were red with tears.

Gracie is a high-energy, athletic creature, graceful as the wind, and it was possible that she simply tweaked something. I grew more worried when Gracie refused to climb the stairs to the second floor.

Julee ladled a measure of warm homemade chicken noodle soup into Gracie's bowl. "This always makes her feel better," she said.

I watched Gracie until it was bedtime. I climbed the stairs, hoping she would follow. Gracie just sat on the landing, her eyes pleading and plaintive before she drooped her head and I disappeared into the bedroom.

A minute later, I reappeared at the top of the stairs, holding my pillow and a blanket. Gracie raised her head. Her tail wagged slowly at the sight of my bedding. She understood I was coming down to sleep with her. She knew she would be safe. That's all she needed from me. That's all so many animals need from us humans. To know that we are there for them, just as they are so often there for us.

I pulled Gracie's bed next to the couch, and we settled in for the night. She gave a satisfied sigh. In the morning we both felt better, and in a few days she was running like the wind again.

Edward Grinnan

Father, You brought my dog into my life to help teach me to be a better human. I think it's working.

A Battle of Wills

"Father, if you are willing, take this cup from me; yet not my will, but yours be done."
—LUKE 22:42 (NIV)

My dachshund, Snuggles, and I have a daily battle of wills over the timing of his walk. Sometimes he wins, sometimes I win—but he never goes down without a fight. The battle goes something like this: Snuggles strategically positions himself between me and the TV, bounces to his back haunches, extends his squat little legs as stabilizers, and glares at me until I surrender. It's very effective.

Recently, in a similar staring match, I realized that I had been looking at my heavenly Father in the same way. My will set, my desire clear in every prayer, I was sure God would yield to my timing. I thought I had tenacious faith, but in reality, it was simply willful stubbornness.

That's when my God lovingly reminded me of the moment when Jesus stared at His Father and begged that the cup be taken from Him. Even the Son of God had to come to a place of surrender. It wasn't that God didn't love His Son, or that He doesn't love me, but my willfulness wasn't in line with His heart for my life.

He had something so much better than fulfilling my immediate desire—and to see it, I, too, had to surrender.

On rare occasions, when Snuggles surrenders, he flops back to earth and climbs into my lap. In that moment, his will comes into line with my heart for him: I will take him on a walk, but for now, I want to love on him and be at peace together. And that is God's heart for me as well. Everything flows from those moments when I climb into His lap, lay down my agenda, and realize that faith is a place of surrender, where we take Him at His word and trust that His timing is best.

Tracy Joy Jones

God, I surrender to Your will today. You know the desires of my heart, and You know the good things You have for me. Help me to rest in Your perfect love today and trust Your timing. Amen.

A Home for Harry

For here we do not have an enduring city, but we are looking for the city that is to come.
—HEBREWS 13:14 (NIV)

Harry was perfect. When he would let us cuddle him in rare, sleepy moments—exhausted from running around the house, harness clenched between his teeth—he resembled a big teddy bear. He was a black and brown goldendoodle with a brilliant white patch on his chest, and he was the spunkiest puppy I'd ever known.

And he would be leaving all too soon.

We'd had him for only four days, but Harry had quickly filled up our hearts. We were watching him while my friend and her husband were in the hospital, where she was having a baby. Still, in many ways it seemed Harry had already become a part of our family.

The afternoon Harry's "father," Anthony, came to pick him up, we gave him our hugs and said our goodbyes. The sweet little pup who had filled our home with energy would no more be ours. With his dreaded harness and leash on, Harry poked his nose out the door to see his true caretaker. I don't think I could have imagined a more touching reunion. Anthony knelt on the mat of my front porch, while Harry placed his paws on either side of Anthony's neck, hug-like, licking his face and giving small jumps. I fought tears, because as much fun as Harry had had at our home, there was definitely no place like *his* home and *his* father.

As Anthony and Harry drove away, I was surprised at the peace that came upon me. I'd expected to be sad, but instead, Harry reuniting with his father just felt right. Thanks to Harry, I was reminded of how *right* home was for each of us. In many ways, I'm confident this is how I'll feel once I reach heaven—that everything will just be right, perfect. I will be truly home.

Heidi Chiavaroli

***Lord, thanks for watching over me until
I can come home to You.***

A Good-Night Ritual

Dear friends, since God so loved us, we also ought to love one another.
—1 JOHN 4:11 (NIV)

When it comes time to say good night, my husband, Mike, has his own little ritual. First, he goes to Petey, our young golden retriever, and pats him softly on the head. "Ernest loves you, Mom loves you, I love you, and God loves you." Petey blinks his eyes and rolls onto his back for a belly rub.

Then Mike approaches eleven-year-old golden retriever Ernest, curled up on his blanket by the foot of our bed, and repeats the blessings. "Petey loves you, Mom loves you, I love you, and God loves you." Ernest places his paw on Mike's arm, pinning him down, in an attempt to keep him there longer. Mike obliges because Ernest is that sweet.

Although they clearly love the attention, there's no way to know for sure how much Petey and Ernest get out of this ritual. But Mike says that he feels something special when he does it. Maybe it is, in part, the security of checking in with all the members of our family, making sure they're all right before laying his own head on the pillow. Or the comfort of the nightly routine. But in addition, he says, a calmness settles over him, a feeling that God is among us, taking care of all our needs.

Of course, no one in the family is left out. Every night Mike hugs me tight. "Petey loves you, Ernest loves you, I love you, and God loves you."

I feel it too. God is there with us. Good night.

Peggy Frezon

Each evening when I say a prayer, how glad I am that You are there. I feel Your presence everywhere, and not a pup escapes your care. Amen.

Freedom within Bounds

Stand fast therefore in the liberty by which Christ has made us free, and do not be entangled again with a yoke of bondage.
—GALATIANS 5:1 (NKJV)

Marcus is a loving and cheerful pet. He greets us with joy each morning, remains polite to a fault, and encourages us to get plenty of exercise. A golden retriever, Marcus couldn't be more well-behaved in the house these days, but it wasn't always that way.

When he came to us as a young rescue, Marcus showed his abundant energy several times a day. The mailman sent him barking and jumping in all directions. Any noise outside launched Marcus; he raced through the house with comic and sometimes costly consequences. On one of his romps, he knocked over a vase and a potted plant on his way to answer the door.

After consulting with several dog-owner friends, we realized that Marcus needed more exercise than we had time to provide via walks. So we installed a six-foot fence around our large backyard. Within a few days, the resourceful pup dug a hole beneath the barrier and found his way into our neighbor's pool. Almost at wit's end, we installed an electronic fence. A fast learner, Marcus quickly caught on. Now, he safely races around our yard and enjoys carefree exercise.

God uses fences in my life too. As a Christian, I have freedom in Christ, but God loves me too much to let me run amok. His gentle barriers keep me on the right track and help me find my best place in the world. By trusting in God's grace and love, I am able to enjoy freedom in Jesus and the best that life has to offer.

David L. Winters

Lord, help me recognize the boundaries You've set for me so I can stay on the right path.

Nothing to Fear

Then David said to Solomon his son, "Be strong and courageous and do it. Do not be afraid and do not be dismayed, for the LORD God, even my God, is with you."
—1 CHRONICLES 28:20 (ESV)

Asher's movement was subtle, a slight shift out of my path. I carried a laundry basket through the kitchen, and the dog, who was temporarily staying with us, watched me with his typical panting grin and tail wag. But as someone who had trained and lived with a fearful dog for years, I knew how to spot the slightest signs of fright—and his subtle shift had been one of them.

The visiting dog's owner had said Asher was fearless. After a few days of observing him in our home, though, I noticed he had plenty of fears. He was simply adept at avoiding them. When anyone walked by with a large object, for example, he wouldn't appear frightened to the untrained eye. He just seemed to move out of the way, which is what most people want from a dog when they're carrying heavy things.

In reality, he was giving the laundry basket and other objects a wide berth because they scared him. Avoidance spared him from having to face his fear. As I set down the basket and used treats and praise to teach Asher he had nothing to fear, I realized I'm just like him.

When I admit to people that I'm a fearful person, they're surprised because I don't seem fearful. Like Asher, I'm good at avoiding my fears. It's easy to appear fearless when I go out of my way to avoid what scares me. But when I live my life avoiding fear, I'm letting fear control me by dictating my choices—what I can and cannot do. I'm letting fear win.

I will never conquer any fear unless I face it. Then God, through His goodness and love, will show me I had nothing to fear in the first place.

Jerusha Agen

In Your Word, You tell me not to fear, but to be strong and courageous. Help me remember You are with me wherever I go.

Thirsty

O God, You are my God; early will I seek You; my soul thirsts for You; my flesh longs for You in a dry and thirsty land where there is no water.
—PSALM 63:1 (NKJV)

One cloudy Florida day, we launched our tandem kayak in the Tarpon Bayou. My husband sat in the back, and our Yorkie, Minnie, sat on my lap in the front.

We paddled east along the gentle water, observing the greenery and wildlife. A couple of passing boats rocked us with their wakes. A bridge overhead gave a few minutes' respite after the blazing sun emerged from the clouds.

We spotted a small, secluded beach and aimed for it. A chance to reapply sunscreen and stretch our legs. We pulled the kayak up on the sand. I filled Minnie's water bowl and set it down. After a few licks, she pulled her leash—and me—toward the river. This wasn't like her. Minnie loves sand, not water.

She continued to tug, so I let her lead the way. Minnie went in the water far enough to cover her short legs and plopped on her bottom. Then she stretched herself out and lay down so only her head and the top half of her life jacket peeked above the surface. Once relieved from the heat, she was ready to get out.

Minnie's instincts had kicked in. She was hot, wanted to cool down, and knew just what to do. I wish I did too. I can look to the things of the world to fill my empty places. Although accomplishments and relationships bring me satisfaction, they always leave me wanting more.

Minnie's wet hair refreshed my hot skin as we got in the kayak and paddled to the dock. It was a reminder for my heart that God blesses me with the things I need, even when I don't know what they are.

Crystal Storms

Lord, help me recognize that all I desire is found in You. Fill my thirsty heart with more of You. Amen.

As I Have Loved You

A new commandment I give to you, that you love one another; as I have loved you, that you also love one another.

—JOHN 13:34-35 (NKJV)

I was pushing my shopping cart from the grocery store to my car when a big scraggly dog came bounding toward me. "BUBBA!" the voice of a girl called to him.

A boisterous group of teens raced after the dog, who was now at my side, tongue hanging out and tail wagging. I couldn't resist his bold, unreserved greeting.

A girl from the group spoke. "Bubba loves *everybody*!" She informed me that they were members of a teen ministry from the church across the street. Their youth pastor was waiting in the church van to take them to feed the homeless and forgotten beneath the town's overpasses, and Bubba would be their lead. I had to ask: "So your ministry team is led by a dog?"

"Pastor says he's our canine front man. Bubba's the first one they'll see. He's our ambassador of love!" the girl giggled excitedly. Their four-legged emissary had now moved on to greet a mom and her wide-eyed toddler.

I overheard the group's plans. Their outing was in remembrance of Maundy Thursday, the night before Jesus was crucified on the cross. On this night long ago, Jesus gathered His disciples, washed their feet as an illustration of serving others, then broke bread with them at their last supper together. This was the night when He commanded them to love one another.

I got it. Bubba, the dog, was the perfect representative of Jesus's unconditional love. This spirited, selfless dog opened the hearts of strangers to feel the Lord's heart for them.

I felt Jesus commanding me—using the example of Bubba, the canine ambassador—to reach out to more people with His unconditional love. To be of service to both friends and strangers alike. This would indeed bless others—and as a result, bless my Lord.

Sandra Clifton

It can be hard to reach out, Lord, even when I know I should. Thank You for sending me good examples when I need them.

Thor Grows Up

Listen, my son, to your father's instruction and do not forsake your mother's teaching. They are a garland to grace your head and a chain to adorn your neck.
—PROVERBS 1:8-9 (NIV)

Every neighborhood needs a funny character of a dog whose name doesn't match its breed. Ours is a cocker spaniel named Thor. When I first met Thor, he was a floppy-eared puppy, still tripping over his own paws and getting tangled in his leash. He reminded me of a windup toy. I knew he was coming before I saw him, when I heard his owner gently remind him, "Slow down, Thor. I know, you see a friend. Sit. *Sit.*"

It was tempting to rush over and pet him, even if he hadn't obeyed the "Sit" command (OK, I usually blew it on this one), or to keep petting him even if he playfully nipped at my hand, brushing it off as normal puppy behavior. But that wouldn't help him grow into a well-behaved dog that his family could proudly take out into a community filled with other dogs, children, and neighbors. I didn't have pets anymore, but I was still raising a son and understood the frustration of well-meaning people overriding my authority. That got even more challenging when I became a single mom. No matter how adorable Thor was, I needed to learn when to step back and let his owners train him according to what they knew about his personality and breed. Friends and family had supported me as I learned to trust my instincts and God's direction for my boys. I wanted to be a supportive fellow parent, too, whether my neighbors were raising kids or puppies.

I ran into Thor the week my youngest son, Nathan, graduated from high school. Thor still reminded me of a windup toy, but a calmer, more mature version. Like Nathan, he reflected the rewards of loving instruction—an ongoing process of growth that I was thankful to be part of.

Jeanette Hanscome

Please look after young parents, God, and help their children grow up wise and strong.

The Lady with the Big Black Dog

"I have set you an example that you should do as I have done for you."
—JOHN 13:15 (NIV)

When I was new in town, I would jog through the area yanked along by a huge black canine named Buddy. "So, you're the lady with the big black dog." That was my introductory phrase for several years in Lindstrom, Minnesota. There was nothing wrong with that introduction, but I did have nightmares thinking that "Lady with the big black dog" would be the epitaph on my tombstone. If I had to choose something to be remembered by, I'd rather it be something like, "She loved her family, helped the poor, and tried [emphasis on *tried*] to follow Jesus."

But if I truly want those words as my legacy, I'm going to have to be bolder; I need to outwardly love, generously give, and loudly follow Jesus. The proof that people watch others was in how many recognized me just from my running down the street. That tells me people watch everything we do, be it Christlike or not. So, when I am out and about, I know the example I set will tell others about God.

Buddy was a natural in drawing people to him. Who doesn't like to hug a big old ball of fur! Clearly, I need to learn more from Buddy's example. I need to be approachable, joyous, and kind. God is a natural too, but in His case, it's my job to show God to others. I fear I have a long way to go to be the magnet that Buddy was on our exercise runs.

Linda Bartlett

Father of all, forgive me for the harsh words and thoughtless deeds that I display so often. Draw me closer to You and Your example of how to live. Remind me that I and Your followers are Your hands and feet on earth. Thank You for Your perfect example and the love You give. Amen.

Before you get a dog,
you can't quite imagine
what living with one might be
like; afterward, you can't
imagine living any other way.

CAROLINE KNAPP, AUTHOR

Perfect Forgiveness

Be kind and compassionate to one another; forgiving each other, just as in Christ God forgave you.
—EPHESIANS 4:32 (NIV)

If looks could kill, I'd have been dead twice over. I'd taken Gracie to one of her favorite places—Tractor Supply Company. Gracie has trained the cashiers there to give her treats, planting her big paws on the counter. Smart girl. But I had a secret agenda, and when Gracie perceived my nefarious plan, I got the look.

A bath.

At the rear of the store is a little doggie spa with tubs, shampoo, towels, blow dryers, combs, everything you need to bathe your dog. I've never understood how a dog who loves to roll in mud finds a bath so objectionable. I talk softly to her and ply her with treats, and she still acts as if she's been led to the gallows.

At home, she retires to one of her several beds and shows me her back. Turning their backs is a way dogs sometimes demonstrate that they are upset with you. Today she was particularly adamant in her affect. Even when I brought her a peace offering—a bit of string cheese, her favorite—she snatched it from me without making eye contact.

So, I settled in to watch the Yankees drop another game to the Rays. I was nodding off when I felt a cold nudge on my hand. Gracie. She looked up at me as if to say, "All is forgiven. Let's be friends again."

Forgiveness is difficult. I'm not always as magnanimous as my dog. I can cling to a grudge. Maybe I derive satisfaction in nursing a sense of injustice. Yet I know that forgiveness is a necessary ingredient in a strong faith. Jesus came to earth to forgive our sins. We are expected to forgive.

I scratched behind Gracie's ears, and she laid her head on my knee. It was nice to be friends again.

Edward Grinnan

Lord, You know I have trouble forgiving a wrong. Today help me let go of a resentment and take a step toward You.

A Better Plan

Many are the plans in a person's heart,
but it is the L*ORD****'s purpose that prevails.***
—PROVERBS 19:21 (NIV)

Our only son, Ryan, had been pining for a dog since he was four years old. When he turned seven, my husband and I decided he was ready to take care of a pet. Ryan jumped and squealed with joy when we told him the news. "Let's go get a dog now!" We explained to our son that adopting a dog from a shelter took time and effort.

Expectant and eager, Ryan and I began the search for our first family pet. We visited local animal shelters and contacted dog rescue organizations. We filled out application forms, showed up at adoption events, and prayed every night that we would find the right dog. We had no idea how difficult and time-consuming it would be to find a small adult dog that met our specific criteria. As the days turned into weeks, Ryan's impatience and disappointment grew.

One morning, our family arrived at an adoption event to see Captain, an adorable miniature schnauzer. Ryan had seen Captain's profile online and was convinced that

Captain was the one. But at the event, we saw another family filling out the paperwork to take Captain home. Our son's big eyes welled up. I hugged him, saying, "Be patient. We can trust God." Ryan rubbed his moist eyes with his hands and nodded. We prayed, believing that God will answer our prayers in His time.

Within a few days, we met Kyle, an affectionate two-year-old Maltese mix, at a shelter. He ran straight into Ryan's arms. Kyle checked all our boxes for a family pet, and we adopted him. My husband and I had planned to teach our son responsibility and ownership. But God's plan was to teach him, and us, to wait patiently on Him and trust He always has a better plan.

Mabel Ninan

Dear God, please help us believe that Your plans for us are good. May we learn to trust in Your perfect timing. Grant us patience as we wait on You. Amen.

A Guardian Angel to the Rescue

God is not unjust; he will not forget your work and the love you have shown him as you have helped his people and continue to help them.
—HEBREWS 6:10 (NIV)

Recently, my neighbor told me he was going to get a husky puppy, as he'd always loved huskies. I went home and got online to find out more about their temperament and came across a story about a husky named Nanook.

Nanook lives with his owner near the start of a trail in Alaska's Chugach State Park. The husky was out wandering the trail when he came upon a young deaf woman, who during a three-day hiking trip had tumbled seven hundred feet down a snowy mountain when one of her hiking poles snapped. Nanook spotted her and pulled her to safety.

The husky remained by her side as she continued hiking the trail. And when she slipped and fell again, this time while crossing the strong freezing currents of the Eagle River, Nanook pulled her to dry land by her backpack straps.

To get warm, the woman curled up in her sleeping bag, determined to keep hiking. But Nanook began to lick her face until she finally activated her emergency locator.

After Alaska State Troopers picked them both up, they returned the dog to his owner, who admitted that Nanook often goes wandering off by himself in search of rescue missions. The woman claimed Nanook was a hero—her guardian angel.

"That's a good kind of dog to have," I told my neighbor the next time I saw him.

Nanook got me thinking, though, about ways I can help others and be their "guardian angel." I don't have to be skilled or have credentials or special talents. I just have to love other people enough to help them when they really need it.

Ginger Kolbaba

God, help me keep my eyes and ears open to the opportunities You present me to help others when they most need it. Amen.

Pie Thief

Have mercy upon me, O LORD; for I am weak.
—PSALM 6:2 (KJV)

With pies baked and the smell of succulent turkey filling the air, I glanced out the window and had to laugh. Our sixty-pound golden retriever, Chelsea, was running *backward* across the yard. Nine pumpkin-colored pups followed in hot pursuit, trying to nurse as they ran. Five weeks old, the puppies had eaten dry dog food for a week but still enjoyed frequent milk breaks. However, Chelsea had about had her fill of the whole mothering experience.

I stepped onto the patio, and the harried mother skidded to a stop beside me, her eyes imploring. "All right, I'll bring you in for a little while," I told her. "But you'll have to behave."

After settling her on the laundry-room floor, I went to straighten up the bathrooms before my extended family arrived for dinner. I returned to the kitchen in time to see the pitiful, overworked mother with her paws on the counter, licking up the last of our pumpkin pie.

"Chelsea!" I grabbed her collar and shoved her out the door, all sympathy for her plight gone.

I fumed while baking a new dessert, but a few hours later, I found myself empathizing with my weak-willed dog. Mounds of dressing and mashed potatoes, giblet gravy, and my favorite fruit salad stared me in the face. *Resist* was no longer in my vocabulary. Seconds? Yes! Pie? Of course. How do we battle a day tailor-made for overindulging? I have more in common with my pie thief than I'd like to admit, yet God knows my weaknesses and shows me mercy when I fail. Rather than banish me to my tormentors, as I did Chelsea, He picks me up, dusts me off, and shows me how I can do better. More than anything, I'm thankful for His mercy.

Tracy Crump

When I feel weak, God, I will lean on you for strength, knowing You'll fortify my resolve to battle any enticement.

A Furry Fest

And let us consider how we may spur one another on toward love and good deeds, not giving up meeting together, as some are in the habit of doing, but encouraging one another—and all the more as you see the Day approaching.
—HEBREWS 10:24-25 (NIV)

"Sorry, I'll be out of town," Marie replied to my invitation for an impromptu girls' movie night. "It's time for Yorkie Fest!"

Ah, yes. Who could compete with Yorkie Fest? Certainly not me, no matter how enticing the alternative plan. Marie and her daughter, Anne, had been attending their self-created event for years. Little chance of anyone intruding on that particular weekend. Part of me wanted to be included; it sounded like such fun. But as a Yorkie-less lass, I didn't qualify. That was OK. I knew how much it meant to Marie.

She and her daughter bred Yorkies as a side business. But they sold them at a very low price. That way, the mother-daughter team wielded some control over the animals' futures. The pups were offered first to friends of good repute and, as a result, were easily placed. Providing a safe home and a good life was well worth the loss of profit.

But they also wanted to keep tabs on the puppies. So they invented Yorkie Fest: an all-day gathering of owners and dogs at a friend's expansive home once a year. Attendees brought potluck and puppies, ready to catch up with lunch and laughter. If a holiday was near, the pups might be dressed in costume to celebrate. And dogs could be purchased right on site and go home with their new family. Friendships also deepened as the group that so adored miniature dogs found they loved one another too—in a big way.

It reminded me of another gathering with a singular focus—that of believers who come together in worship to lavish love and praise on God and join one another in fellowship.

Cathy Elliott

May I bring the same enthusiasm to my worship with others as Marie and her daughter bring to Yorkie Fest.

Touchdowns with Duchess

***But the fruit of the Spirit is love, joy, peace,
longsuffering, kindness, goodness, faithfulness.***
—GALATIANS 5:22 (NKJV)

Growing up, I was considered, in polite circles, husky. I was never an athlete, so my interest in sports was minimal. I felt a bit guilty and insecure about that. But I lived in northwest Indiana and was raised Catholic, so watching Notre Dame football games on television was mandatory.

The fall Saturday ritual was to meet at the home of the McConnels and gather in the basement den to watch the game. For me, the biggest draw was the buffet setup—which clues you in to my priorities. I was also very fond of the family pet. Everyone loved Duchess, an overweight boxer dog, who was the elderly canine matriarch of the family of seven children. She benevolently tolerated being dressed up and hugged on and serving as an all-purpose four-legged nanny for the kids.

I always tried to get a seat near where Duchess lay during the game. As the event progressed, Duchess didn't move a muscle. But as soon as the cheers went up for a Notre Dame touchdown, she would jump up and run in circles to celebrate the team triumph, then collapse again to her prone position.

Game after game, year after year, Duchess was there—loved for no other reason than that she was Duchess. It was unconditional and reciprocal love. She always greeted visitors in the same welcoming fashion, and guests reciprocated in kind.

Duchess, in her unique way, taught me the value of kindness and the power of being nonjudgmental. This much-loved boxer was an illustration of compassion and empathy, areas in which, to be honest, I don't always succeed. Still, thanks to Duchess, I know the tangible, powerful, and positive consequences of those virtues. And I came to realize that this attitude of love, kindness, and patience toward others is a demonstrable and powerful expression of God's love for us.

Terry Clifton

Lord, help me to be alert to the examples of love coming from the animals in my life. And let me, in turn, reflect that love to those You bring my way. Amen.

Finn's Sensitive Pace

Let each of you look out not only for his own interests, but also for the interests of others.
—PHILIPPIANS 2:4 (NKJV)

Our black Labrador, Finn, adores the outdoors. He tolerates being with us inside, but all the while his heart longs to lie in the grass on our wooded yard. This makes my husband, Rob, Finn's best friend.

Rob is the yard person in our household. He's a consummate putterer, and yards are wonderful puttering grounds. He putters with plants, cars, grass, gutters, and grandkids. His puttering is productive but leisurely paced. He waters, weeds, trims, and tinkers. He and the grandchildren pick berries, spot birds, and play croquet. Finn revels in the hours he can devote to enjoying the outdoors while Rob goes about his puttering.

Which is why, every day, the moment Rob emerges from our second-floor bedroom, Finn appears at his feet and races Rob down the stairs to the front door. I can almost hear his dog thoughts. *He's up! He's up! We're going outside! I love the outside. We're going outside. Hurry up, Rob! Hurry! The day is waiting!*

Years ago, Rob moved as quickly as Finn, and they created one thundering rush to the yard each morning.

Over time, Rob used the banister more and more, but still they descended in tandem.

In 2013, Rob woke one morning and collapsed. Within two weeks, he was diagnosed with multiple sclerosis. It's hit his balance hard, and I initially worried about his morning ritual with Finn. Rob's stubborn, though, and wouldn't hear of reorienting Finn to sleep downstairs.

In only a couple of weeks, I noticed Finn had made an adjustment on his own. One morning, he waited on the top stair until Rob reached the bottom. Just like that, Finn put Rob's needs ahead of his own and continues the habit to this day.

How does a dog know how to live out love better than many humans? Their daily descent down the stairs is a lovely living picture of Paul's command in Philippians and inspires me to greater love for others.

Lori Stanley Roeleveld

When I forget, Lord, remind me to be as sensitive to the needs and pace of others as Finn is.

Let Go and Let God

Draw near to God, and he will draw near to you. Cleanse your hands, you sinners, and purify your hearts, you double-minded.
—JAMES 4:8 (ESV)

My friend Susanne took her two eight-month-old Lab puppies to a nearby middle school soccer field one afternoon so they all could get some good exercise. The two fifty-pounders were roughhousing as usual when suddenly Otis got his bottom teeth stuck in Maggie's collar, which began to choke her.

Alone with no one else in sight, Susanne did her best to push the two strong dark-brown puppies together to ease the tension so Otis could get his teeth loose, but her attempts probably confused them. Her efforts to push them together must have seemed contradictory. They were trying to get separated, apart, and away from each other.

Though Susanne did not have the physical strength to help save Maggie, she did have something even better—prayer power. Immediately she started praying for the Lord's help in the seemingly impossible crisis: "I need you, God! Maggie needs you! Please help!"

And just as she uttered those desperate words, the Lab puppies became disentangled. "The Lord's power overcame the crisis," she told me later, "and neither dog was hurt."

As I thought about the puppies' life-threatening tug-of-war, I remembered times when I resisted the Lord's pull, only to find myself in a worse mess. During my senior year of college, I sensed God's pull to go into fulltime ministry. But I figuratively pulled away like Jonah did in the Bible. I was stubborn and thought my way was the best way. While I didn't get swallowed by a whale, I did find myself in miserable jobs for years that seemed purposeless.

When I finally stopped resisting God and prayed, "Lord, use me," He graciously led me to inspirational writing—work I could have been doing for the prior dozen years. God knows my heart's desires, even when I cannot articulate them myself. So now I know it's always best to let go and draw near to Him.

Janet Holm McHenry

Lord, use me.

Comfort as You've Been Comforted

Comfort, comfort my people, says your God.
—ISAIAH 40:1 (NIV)

For a Dalmatian that weighed a hundred pounds, you'd never guess Newton was a gentle giant. His gentleness and uncanny ability to empathize with humans was never more on display than the day my cousin Amy visited with her baby.

Not quite sure what to do about a tiny infant in the house, my dog sat beside me with his favorite stuffed toy at his feet. Amy placed Chandler on her blanket on the living room floor, and Newton never took his eyes off the baby. Fascinated as Chandler cooed and laughed, he tilted his head back and forth. When the baby's giggles headed toward fussing, Newton shifted his position. No longer sitting next to me, he now lay at my feet.

As the volume of Chandler's distress increased, Newton inched his way toward her on his belly, his favorite stuffy in his mouth. When he neared the edge of Chandler's blanket, Newton placed his toy on the floor. He gently nudged it toward her with his nose.

Instantly, the fussing stopped. Before Chandler reached for Newton's stuffed animal, I retrieved it. At the same time, Amy picked up her child.

With Newton seated beside me once more, I returned his favorite stuffy to him. As I stroked his head, I marveled at his empathy and willingness to share something so precious. That day, my dog saw a need and moved to fill it. He noticed someone in distress, and offered up what he had to ease their pain. Through Newton, God showed me I need to be as willing as my dog to do the same.

Sandy Kirby Quandt

Father, I pray You will move in me so I can see the needs of those You put in my path. Give me a willingness to comfort as You have comforted me. Amen.

Loving Ernest-ly

"Which of these three do you think was a neighbor to the man who fell into the hands of robbers?" The expert in the law replied, "The one who had mercy on him." Jesus told him, "Go and do likewise."

—LUKE 10:36-37 (NIV)

The woman sat at a picnic table outside a McDonald's, wearing layers of heavy sweaters despite the August heat. Two tattered trash bags and a backpack, with a coat and blanket tied to the top, lay at her feet. I imagined these were all her worldly possessions.

We were returning from a trip. "We had better walk the dogs away from there," I said.

My husband went inside to get food, while I took the dogs and headed away from the picnic-table lady. However, my golden retriever, Ernest, strained at the leash and pulled with all of his eighty-five pounds. This wasn't like him, a mellow fellow. But he tugged me right toward the woman I was trying to avoid.

I struggled with myself. Why was I turning away from her? Didn't God teach us to love one another? Shouldn't I show her kindness and compassion? With Ernest leading the way, I finally approached the woman.

"Hi!" I said.

"He's not going to bite?" she asked.

"Oh no," I said. "Are you having a nice day?"

She looked at us curiously. "You know?" she said. "I guess I am."

I wasn't sure what to do or what she needed. "Well," I said, smiling. "I just wanted to say hi. Ernest here suggested I come over."

"He did?" Her eyes grew wide. I could tell she wasn't exactly a dog person, but her gaze softened. "No one ever says hi to me. Thank you, Ernest."

As we walked away, I knew I had done the right thing. But I couldn't take all the credit. It was Ernest's idea.

Peggy Frezon

Dear Father, teach me how to be compassionate to those I meet. If they need help, show me what I can do. If they need attention, give me the words. Thank You.

> Everyone thinks they have the best dog. And none of them are wrong.
>
> W. R. PURSCHE, AUTHOR

Held in His Loving Arms

But let all who take refuge in you be glad. . . .
Spread your protection over them.
—PSALM 5:11 (NIV)

"What's Gracie barking at?" Julee said.

I jogged down to the apple tree. Our golden had treed a small, dark creature now curled at the top branch. *Probably a black squirrel,* I thought.

"C'mon, Cujo, you made your point."

Gracie pranced up the hill behind me, casting an occasional woof over her shoulder. Dogs. Always have to have the last word. When it was time for bed, Gracie came over to me, limping slightly. She sat and showed me her paw. There were thin, silvery quills mixed in with her golden fur. That was a porcupine she'd treed, probably a youngster.

I dug out some pain pills she'd had for a strained back. I wanted her to sleep deeply enough so she wouldn't chew the quills and have one end up in her throat. I'd take her to the vet first thing tomorrow.

In the morning, Gracie's veterinarian, Dr. Phillips, said she would try to remove the quills without sedation. My whole body tensed as they led Gracie to the treatment room. I stood there holding her leash and begging God to please, please, please not let it hurt. It seemed like hours before they brought her back.

"How is she?"

"Amazing. She didn't flinch; she didn't even yelp. We must have pulled out thirty quills." She showed me the quills floating in a surgical dish. My knees went weak. They sent Gracie home with antibiotics and a new toy.

Did God keep her in His arms while they took out the quills? I like to keep that image in my imagination and in my heart. I have a brave dog and a loving God.

Edward Grinnan

God of love, You love all creatures. Thank You for watching over our dogs—and the porcupines too.

Tiny but Tough

***This is how love is made complete among us so that
we will have confidence on the day of judgment:
In this world we are like Jesus. There is no fear in love.
But perfect love drives out fear.***

—1 JOHN 4:17-18 (NIV)

When our son and his family went on vacation, we babysat our "granddogs." Minnie and Georgia are tiny but tough—vocally anyway. No one would dare harm us when these two are around. They bark when someone knocks on the door. They bark when my husband walks into the kitchen. They bark when the popcorn starts popping in the microwave. I feel so safe.

One day, I let the two terrors out to run in our fenced-in backyard. A few minutes later, ferocious barking erupted in front of the house. I walked outside to find that our little Houdini, a.k.a. Georgia, had slipped under the gate and run across the street. There she stood, dressing down our neighbor in his own front yard. Georgia didn't back off until I ordered her home in a none-too-patient voice. "I'm sorry," I called, waving to our neighbor. "She thinks she's tough stuff."

He laughed. "I feared for my life."

The thing is, I know Georgia's not really as brave or aggressive as she appears. In fact, when I reach down to pet her, she flattens her ears and ducks. One sharp word and she heads to her kennel. Most of the time, she barks in fear.

I wonder how many people who bark at me are reacting out of fear—or sorrow or anger. Their outbursts may have nothing to do with me. Runaway emotions can cause someone to act in ways that hurt other people. When I respond in kind, it only makes the situation worse. But I have an antidote: love. When I reply as Jesus would, love cancels out fear. Maybe not right away, but eventually. God's love is bigger and tougher than anything fear can produce.

Tracy Crump

The next time someone barks at me, help me bite back that cutting reply and find something encouraging to say.

Gifting

Every good and perfect gift is from above.
—JAMES 1:17 (NIV)

Scuppers, our newly adopted dog, glanced tentatively at the stuffed squeaky toy we had given him. He timidly approached it while repeatedly glancing back at us.

Poor little dog, I thought. *He thinks we're going to snatch the toy from him.* If only he would realize that we love giving him gifts and want him to enjoy them.

I used to be like Scuppers when thinking about God. I was convinced that He was going to snatch back any gift or blessing He had given me. I imagined that there was a certain amount of time or quota of blessings that one received and once the ration was used, that was it. Eventually one's blessings were depleted, and troubles would emerge.

During our first years of marriage, I was convinced something horrible would occur because I was so happy. At one point I worked myself into crying fits, convinced that my blessings of a healthy life with a loving husband would come to an end. At that time in my life, I was working with terminally ill cancer patients, and I was convinced every little ache and pain was something deadly. Instead of thoroughly enjoying my marital moments, I continually worried about my situation.

Eventually I came to the conclusion that my marriage was a gift from God and that He is not a God who is spiteful or mean spirited. He wants to bless us with gifts like a loving marriage and good health. He is not planning to snatch them from our grasp. He wants us to relax and enjoy those gifts.

God is good. He wants nothing more than to give us His best. Just as we want Scuppers to take the toys we give him and to enjoy them, God wants us to receive His gifts.

Virginia Ruth

God, help me trust that the gifts You give are real and that they will last.

Penitent Pooch

***Whoever heeds life-giving correction will be
at home among the wise.***
—PROVERBS 15:31 (NIV)

I caught my dog with his nose in the trash. "No!" I said. A pause, then another reprimand for good measure: "No!" We must have presented an interesting study in body language, the two of us. Me, hands on hips, foot tapping. Him, head bowed, tail between his legs. "I love you, but if you eat garbage, you'll get sick," I said, as though he could understand me.

The thing is, he acted as though he *did* understand me. He walked slowly to me, almost creeping. He stopped at my feet, his chin on his front paws. He looked up at me, chastened and contrite, as if to say, *You're right. My bad.* I found myself thinking: *If I accepted rebuke and criticism that way, it would probably do me good.*

When I am criticized, when someone finds fault with my actions, I immediately get defensive. I feel like I'm being attacked, and I instinctively launch a counterattack. I get angry. I think hurtful thoughts about the person who has corrected me. I can feel the needle on my inner stress-o-meter climbing into the danger zone. I feel bad, physically, emotionally, spiritually. My relationship with the other person is derailed. My relationship with my heavenly Father is derailed.

Lately, I'm trying a new approach: I'll agree with criticism. Not always, but now and then, when criticized, I'll simply say, "You know, you're right. My bad." I'm not talking about becoming a spineless jellyfish. I'm not talking about becoming a doormat and allowing people to walk all over me. But I have found that agreeing with criticism immediately defuses the situation, aborts my counterattack impulse, and enables me to learn something about myself by trying to understand another person's point of view, even if I don't fully agree with it. Best of all, I'm feeling free of the anger that used to arise in me when criticized, the anger that clouded my soul, disrupted my prayer life, and made it downright difficult to love my neighbor.

Louis Lotz

Lord, have there been times when I reacted badly to criticism when I should have listened? Give me the wisdom to take a deep breath when I need to.

Safely Hidden

*You are my hiding place;
you will protect me from trouble.*
−PSALM 32:7 (NIV)

My mom had seven kids and wasn't terribly excited about the prospect of also taking care of pets. Our home was animal-free for several years before a golden retriever named Rusty showed up. He was a lot bigger than the dachshund from my very early years, and Mom did not like to allow him inside the house.

Dad took it upon himself to build a wonderful doghouse for Rusty in the crawl space under the back steps. It wasn't long before I realized that this was a great place to hide when the neighbor kids were playing hide and seek. It was sufficiently tucked away, and not easily discovered by whoever was "It."

It was also a very good hiding place when I needed solitude, a secret refuge where I could retreat from whatever hurt or fear had impacted my little life. I remember withdrawing to this secluded spot several times, and I especially remember the time when Rusty was already there when I crawled inside. He didn't growl or bark or make any other motions that would indicate that he wanted me to leave. In fact, he seemed to know that I was hurting. He let me curl up beside him. He gave me doggie kisses, and let me rest my head on his tummy.

I've heard of people being the hands and feet of Jesus, but on that day, Rusty was the arms of Jesus, comforting me with his sweet presence, loving me through my troubles. He welcomed me into his space and waited patiently for my heart to find rest and peace. He was the embodiment of the Holy Spirit, the Comforter whose name I didn't know yet.

Liz Kimmel

Lord, help me find a safe place to hide away when I need it—one where I can always find Your comfort.

207

Ernest under the Table

***"And surely I am with you always,
to the very end of the age."***
—MATTHEW 28:20 (NIV)

As he's aged, my golden retriever Ernest has developed some quirks. The most puzzling one is his propensity for lying under the coffee table and whining.

One evening I crouched on the floor next to Ernest, stroking his neck. At twelve years old, he seemed fragile and a little lost. I struggled to figure out why he was whining. His vet checkup had been fine. Ernest wasn't there by accident—he'd put himself under the table purposefully. And he wasn't stuck—when he wanted to, he could scoot right out. Yet I felt bad hearing him whine. He seemed to need my attention.

I tried to coax him out from under the table. "Ernest, here!" I just wanted him to trust me.

Instead, my younger golden, Pete, came to me when I called. He sat beside me and looked right into my eyes. When I told him to lie down, he was obedient. He nudged my arm, begging for my attention.

This is how I feel, sometimes, in my walk with Jesus. When I am obedient and things are going well, I may feel like He is ignoring me. I should instead realize that He is there, loving me and rejoicing in my obedience. Yet, when I am lost or hurting, He is there also, crouching beside me. He wants me to trust Him, so that in challenging times He can coax me out from under the table. How grateful I am that He is with me always and loves me in good times and bad.

I called again. Pete leaned closer, Ernest crept forward, and I hugged them both.

Peggy Frezon

Help me to always feel Your presence, Lord, in the times when I feel lost or far from You.

The Best Squeaker

"You shall not covet your neighbor's house; you shall not covet your neighbor's wife, or his male servant, or his female servant, or his ox, or his donkey, or anything that is your neighbor's."
—EXODUS 20:17 (ESV)

The Great Pyrenees and the Leonberger puppy—who was already as big as the Pyr—watched me intently. I picked up two cylindrical squeakers—the remains of destroyed toys—and made my way toward the dogs.

My Leonberger pup, Galen, whined with excitement as he anticipated what I was about to do. Marshmallow, my Great Pyrenees, got into position. I dashed around Galen, throwing a squeaker down the hallway of the house. Galen bounded to retrieve his toy.

Meanwhile, I chucked the other squeaker a shorter distance for Marshmallow to snatch up before Galen could return. But Galen stopped short of his squeaker and came tearing back, trying to steal Marshmallow's toy. Marshmallow prevailed, grabbing his squeaker just before Galen could seize it. Marshmallow triumphantly jogged to his dog bed where he lay down to squeak his prize.

I picked up Galen's squeaker and squeezed it to distract him from Marshmallow. Galen tore his gaze from Marshmallow to look at the squeaker I held. I threw it, and he started toward it. But then he stopped and turned back, the pull of Marshmallow and the forbidden squeaker greater than the toy Galen could have.

I couldn't believe that, even with identical toys, Galen was so obsessed with wanting what he didn't have that he couldn't enjoy what he did have. But I soon realized I can be just as ridiculous. I have an abundance of gifts in my life. Yet I easily become so obsessed with what I don't have—a bigger house, more leisure time, the newest devices—that I miss enjoying what God has given me. When I focus on being grateful for the gifts I have, I can enjoy them and appreciate their uniqueness. Perfect gifts chosen for me by my Creator and Father in heaven.

Jerusha Agen

Help me see the beauty in the gifts that You've given me— and not to pay so much attention to other people's toys.

Taking That First Step

Wait for the LORD; be strong and take heart and wait for the LORD.
—PSALM 27:14 (NIV)

Sometimes I run kicking and screaming when I'm told to do something. Other times, I jump in but feel resentful. Or I start out compliant but then rebel.

That is what our elderly dog Duke did after he was diagnosed with several eye problems by his veterinary ophthalmologist. At our first visit, we learned he was having eye pain—enough that his third eyelid had closed. (I didn't even know dogs had such a thing!) The vet prescribed multiple eye drops to be given every few hours for several weeks.

Duke did great at first. I think the drops eased his pain, so he stood there and let me hold open his eyelids. But after the first week or so, he got tired of me messing with him. He quit complying and would stubbornly slam his eyes shut. Or he would jerk his head away. Eventually, he began running from me anytime I got near. Smart fellow.

His reaction reminds me of a child who doesn't want his teeth brushed. Or a teen who doesn't want to do her homework. Or an adult who dreads going to work . . . or who dreads putting eye drops in an uncooperative pup's eyes.

It also reminds me of myself, when I know God wants me to do something I don't have the time, the courage, or the desire to do. But just as Duke's eye drops were what he needed for healing, sometimes the jobs God has for me end up being exactly what I need at the time. Often, I only see this in hindsight. But I won't know until I step up and try.

Missy Tippens

I want to come to You with courage and a willing heart, God. Please be patient with me when I'm feeling stubborn.

Saving Hercules

If you confess with your mouth the Lord Jesus and believe in your heart that God has raised Him from the dead, you will be saved.
—ROMANS 10:9 (NKJV)

My dad was as tough as they come, but he had a heart that melted like chocolate on a hot sidewalk when it came to kids and animals. He was especially softhearted toward his dog, Hercules, or "my little buddy," as Dad called him.

Dad and his terrier mix were inseparable. They watched football together. Snuck ice cream together. Took long rides around town and hung out in the yard making friends with wild rabbits (or trying to, at least). When my mom traveled, Dad always had her "talk to Hercules" on the phone so he would know "Mom was OK."

One day, two little boys visited and were upset because someone had told them that their pet cats wouldn't go to heaven when they died. That person had been quite certain of this, and the boys were inconsolable, thinking they'd never see their pets again.

I didn't think Dad had even been listening, but when I visited him a week later, he was eager to show me what Hercules could do. The dog sat at Dad's feet, and when Dad asked him, "Hercules, do you love Jesus?"

Hercules barked back three times.

"Dad, are you trying to save your dog?"

He got tears in his eyes. "I know I'll go to heaven, but I can't imagine being there without my little buddy."

Dad and I talked for a long time about God's love for us and for animals, the new heaven and earth, and that we're promised there will be no tears in heaven. We discussed God's character and trustworthiness. He hugged Hercules. "Did you hear all that, little buddy? We can trust God to take care of us, can't we?"

Hercules barked three times and licked Dad's face. I think he knew that lesson all along.

Lori Stanley Roeleveld

I know there will be no more tears in heaven, God. Please help those who aren't so sure.

The Gift of Tranquility

"Be still, and know that I am God."
—PSALM 46:10 (NIV)

Gracie, my golden, is curled up sleeping on the couch while I work. Outside the wind sways the trees, causing the winter sunlight slanting through the west window to ripple across her. We just got back from a cold, snowy hike in the hills of western Massachusetts. She plowed through drifts and vaulted over fallen trees. Plunged her snout into snowbanks, seeking out some scent I could only guess at. At the summit, she sat and leaned into me, staring out past the tree line at the distant, snow-covered, checkerboard farm fields, fences half-buried.

I can't help but stare at her now. She is so peaceful, so serenely relaxed. I doubt I have ever achieved such a state of complete rest. My mind is too restless, as if my brain paces even when I am sitting. I envy this dog and her gift of tranquility.

Deep, slow breaths rise and fall in her chest in a hypnotic rhythm. I try to mirror her, syncing my breathing with hers. As the minutes pass, I feel a peace come over me, as if I am tapping into her serenity. I relax, internally and externally, body and soul. I experience something like spiritual equilibrium rippling through me.

Not everyone has a dog. Not everyone has loved one. For most of my life, I have. For us dog lovers, they teach us to live intentionally, to live with gratitude and optimism (is there a creature more optimistic than a dog?), to find peace in the stillness of the moment.

In a minute, my mind will turn itself back on and I will go back to work. For now, I want to breathe with Gracie, to achieve that state of being completely present, at peace in the moment.

Edward Grinnan

Almighty God, You are pure spirit. Help me to meet You in the moment, to breathe in Your spirit, to close my eyes and find You within.

Acknowledgments

Every attempt has been made to credit the sources of copyrighted material used in this book. If any such acknowledgment has been inadvertently omitted or miscredited, receipt of such information would be appreciated.

Scripture quotations marked (ESV) are taken from *The Holy Bible, English Standard Version.* Copyright © 2001 by Crossway Bibles, a division of Good News Publishers. Used by permission. All rights reserved.

Scripture quotations marked (KJV) are taken from the *King James Version of the Bible.*

Scripture quotations marked (MSG) are taken from *The Message.* Copyright © 1993, 2002, 2018 by Eugene H. Peterson.

Scripture quotations marked (NASB) are taken from the *New American Standard Bible®*, Copyright © 1960, 1971, 1977, 1995, 2020 by The Lockman Foundation. All rights reserved.

Scripture quotations marked (NET) are taken from the *NET Bible®* (New English Translation). Copyright © 1996–2017 by Biblical Studies Press, L.L.C.; http://netbible.com. All rights reserved.

Scripture quotations marked (NIV) are taken from *The Holy Bible, New International Version®, NIV®.* Copyright © 1973, 1978, 1984, 2011 by Biblica, Inc. Used by permission. All rights reserved worldwide.

Scripture quotations marked (NKJV) are taken from the *New King James Version*®. Copyright © 1982 by Thomas Nelson. Used by permission. All rights reserved.

Scripture quotations marked (NLT) are taken from the *Holy Bible, New Living Translation.* Copyright © 1996, 2004, 2007, 2015 by Tyndale House Foundation. Used by permission of Tyndale House Publishers Inc., Carol Stream, Illinois. All rights reserved.

A Note from the Editors

We hope you enjoyed *Faithful Paws,* published by Guideposts. For more than seventy-five years, Guideposts, a nonprofit organization, has been driven by a vision of a world filled with hope. We aspire to be the voice of a trusted friend, a friend who makes you feel more hopeful and connected.

By making a purchase from Guideposts, you join our community in touching millions of lives, inspiring them to believe that all things are possible through faith, hope, and prayer. Your continued support allows us to provide uplifting resources to those in need. Whether through our communities, websites, apps, or publications, we inspire our audiences, bring them together, and comfort, uplift, entertain, and guide them. Visit us at guideposts.org to learn more.

We would love to hear from you. Write us at Guideposts, P.O. Box 5815, Harlan, Iowa 51593 or call us at (800) 932-2145. Did you love *Faithful Paws*? Leave a review for this product on guideposts.org/shop. Your feedback helps others in our community find relevant products.

Find inspiration, find faith, find Guideposts.

Shop our best sellers and favorites at
guideposts.org/shop
Or scan the QR code to go directly to our Shop.